MURDER at
ROCKY POINT PARK

TRAGEDY IN RHODE ISLAND'S SUMMER PARADISE

KELLY SULLIVAN PEZZA

THE
History
PRESS

Published by The History Press
Charleston, SC 29403
www.historypress.net

First published 2014

ISBN 978.1.5402.2362.3

Library of Congress CIP data applied for.

For my babies, Tatiana Maryhelen Pezza and Josef Roland Pezza.
I love you.

CONTENTS

ACKNOWLEDGEMENTS

I am eternally grateful to Greg Pezza, Marylou Fiske, Helen and Roland Baton, Page Sullivan, Mary McCrea and A.J. Nausch of Pawcatuck; the staff and patrons of the Bottom Line Bar in Warwick; Mark Sand of Mystic; the wonderfully helpful staff at the Warwick Town Hall; Kathleen Madrid, Carol Graziano, Steve Grimes, John Davis, Katherine Lowenstrom, Larry Webster, Hope Andrews, Charlie Wright, Lorraine Arruda, Jane Mahoney, Eric White, Matt Wunsch and the staff of Southern Rhode Island Newspapers; Pam Lavoie of Jules Antiques & General Store; and my beautiful children, who taught me how much love the human heart is capable of holding.

INTRODUCTION

From my days as a child, accompanying my grandfather to dusty antique stores or tagging along behind my mother as she did gravestone rubbings, I have been enthralled by history. From this early age, it was instilled in me to have a great love and respect for all things past.

My interest in true crime cannot be as easily explained. Perhaps it is the same adrenalin-inducing addiction that caused my great-grandfather to lose himself in detective novels or that led my grandfather, and later myself, to become involved in law enforcement. When I found it difficult to choose between pursuing my interest in true crime, devoting myself to my love of history or taking advantage of the literary ability I had been given, I luckily found a way to combine all three.

Seventeen years ago, I began working as a newspaper journalist, writing a weekly column on historic local crimes and unsolved mysteries. This necessitated poring over old records, letters, diaries and newspapers for hours every night. On one particular evening, I ventured to the library at the University of Rhode Island to go over its old newspaper collection, in the hopes of finding a lead on a new article. I had been browsing over the reels of microfilm for only a few minutes when my eyes began to hurt, and I decided that I'd locate just one page of interesting material, print it out and call it a night. The moment I noticed an old article bearing the name of a local town alongside the word "murder," I printed out the page without even reading it. I figured it might be interesting or it might not, but I would read it the next morning after my headache had departed.

When my rested eyes later moved over the words on the paper, I realized I didn't have the makings of an article. I had the foundation of a book. The story was shocking, and as a historian, I was amazed that I'd never heard it before. A local man had bludgeoned his little girl at everyone's favorite Rhode Island amusement park. There had been thousands of articles and stories written about the park; why had none of them ever mentioned Maggie Sheffield?

My ensuing research was not easy, not only because the case received very little news coverage and a fire had allegedly burned most of the official records, but also because I found it hard to remain professional. Over the years, I had researched hundreds of murders—terrible, sickening, unspeakable murders. But like a doctor must keep a professional distance from his patients, I had always been able to keep myself from having any emotional feeling toward the people I wrote about. This time, I couldn't do that for some reason.

I was kept awake at night by visions of Maggie in my head, of her last moments and what they must have been like for her. It filled me with despair to write about this child and try to come to terms with the fact that I would never know what she had been thinking as she looked up at her father that day. I could only imagine, and it pained me to imagine it. Very unprofessionally, I cried for Maggie more than a few times.

As I always do when writing about someone deceased, I went to see Maggie's grave. Kneeling there at the small stone engraved with the name "Maggie Segur Sheffield," I swallowed the lump in my throat and reached out to touch it. She was only six feet away from me—this innocent child I had researched, written about, ached for, cried over. She was right here. And this was as close as I could ever get to her.

My connection with Maggie was unlike any I had ever experienced with a research subject before. I felt angered that there seemed to have been more concern for Frank Sheffield than there had been for his daughter. Reporters had not been horrified enough to report on the case any more than necessary, and the memories of her seemed to be extinguished almost as quickly as her life was. I felt driven, more than one hundred years later, to tell her story, her whole story, to make certain her life and death are never forgotten. Perhaps my endeavor was to create the mournful feeling of loss that should have been felt at the time of her unspeakable death.

I know that I will never forget her. In my memory, she is safe. When I returned to visit her grave for a second time, I left for her the last thing she ever asked for in her earthly life. At Rocky Point that fateful day, she had requested that her father give her his handkerchief so that she might tie it into the shape of a doll. Beside a dozen pink carnations, I placed a doll against her gravestone. "Sleep peacefully, angel," I whispered. "Your story will be told."

1

THE MURDER

I Have Killed My Daughter

All the laughter and gay chatter of the massive crowd drifted on the salt air toward the ledges. However, strangely, those sounds seemed to be enveloped somewhere in the center of the music. It was not too far in the distance that carousels and flying swings and roller coasters and train rides rang with the melody of barrel organs.

Closer by, there was only one sound that seemed real, and that was the gentle sound made by the rippling water that lapped against the slippery rocks, slapping them softly before quickly retreating back and dispersing into the vast Atlantic Ocean.

The gaiety and the cheerful din, the music and the ocean, what was real and what was not real all swirling together in amplified chaos—this is what Frank Sheffield heard for a moment. Then he bent down and picked up a large rock that had crumbled from the tall, jagged ledge behind him. He turned to face his five-year-old daughter. The next sound he heard was a scream.

Two young couples, sitting on a knoll not far from the ledge, had been enjoying the beautiful summer day there at Rocky Point Amusement Park in Warwick, Rhode Island. They were immediately startled by the chilling sound that had come from the other side of the ledge, shattering the peaceful atmosphere. One of the boys, Arthur Skirron, quickly got up and rushed toward the area from which the scream had come. When he was about halfway there, Frank came out from behind the ledge, looked at Skirron and then kept right on walking without uttering a single word.

Well aware that something horrific had probably just taken place, Skirron didn't stop to talk to Frank but instead continued on toward the ledge. Once there, he peered over the rocky edge, shock befalling him at what he saw there. Skirron stared in horror. A little girl lay still on the ground, a pool of blood surrounding her. Neatly clad in a pretty dress and shoes, her head was crushed terribly. A gaping hole on the upper part of her forehead continued to gush blood as it accumulated in a scarlet mass on the ground around her small body. Unbelievably, the child was still alive.

Having no idea what type of terrible accident might have just occurred, Skirron nervously hurried toward the main office of the park. Once he arrived there, he notified the park manager, thirty-nine-year-old Randall Augustus Harrington, that a child was severely injured on the northwestern section of the grounds.

A twenty-one-year-old house painter named Robert J. Quinn was standing nearby as Skirron talked and happened to overhear the conversation. Going along with Harrington, he rushed to the scene, where they found the little girl unconscious but still breathing.

With no time to waste, the two men gently but quickly picked the small, limp body up off the hard ground and carried it into the nearest building, which was the park's large theater. They immediately summoned a doctor for help. However, it took twenty minutes for medical assistance to arrive, and by that time, the young life before them had already slipped away.

Leaving his daughter dying painfully on the ground, Frank Sheffield had calmly walked out of the park and begun heading in the direction of the nearby Warwick Club, a private association of local jewelry manufacturers and other successful businessmen. Once in the club's parking lot, he approached fifty-five-year-old Newell Warren Belcher, a hardware dealer from Providence, and another man named Daniel Remington.

"I want to be turned over to an officer," Frank boldly announced to the men. "I have killed my child."

Belcher and Remington were totally unprepared to hear such an utterance come from the stranger's mouth. They weren't sure what to think as Frank went on.

"Why I did it, I don't know. I did not know that I had done anything until I had killed her. I did not know I had struck her until I saw the blood."

At that point, Frank suddenly began to shake quite badly and act in a manner so strange that Belcher and Remington believed the person before them was simply a victim of insane delusions, spouting out words that had no basis in reality. However, when Frank made his request again, asking that he be turned over to authorities, the men figured it was better to be safe than sorry and complied with his wishes.

They walked him back onto the grounds of Rocky Point Park and delivered him into the custody of manager Harrington, who also happened to be a police constable.

They reported what Frank had just told them, and as Harrington had just left the scene of the dreadful crime and witnessed the agonizing death that followed, he immediately placed Frank under arrest. While awaiting transportation to the county jail, Frank was held in the lockup cell that was kept on the grounds of the park.

News of the terrible tragedy that had just occurred made its way around the busy amusement park quickly. Suddenly, most of the visitors at the park that day were much more interested in learning about the grisly details of the murder than they were in popcorn, cymbal-playing monkeys or famed trapeze performer Madame Zoe. It was later reported that Zoe herself had conversed with patrons about the shocking event and stated that whoever killed the child should be hanged by the neck.

While awaiting the arrival of police officers, Harrington returned to the bloody scene near the water. There, he retrieved a broken piece of ledge that was lying on the ground and that he assumed could very well be the murder weapon. The club-like piece was nearly ten inches long and two inches wide on one end. The other end was tapered to a point with square edges. The thicker portion was smeared with Maggie's blood, and strands of the little girl's hair had adhered to it.

Sitting in the park's cell, Frank began to act extremely nervous. This soon gave way to his behavior becoming completely bizarre. Repeatedly, he asked aloud why he had committed the deplorable act that had resulted in the death of his daughter. Each time he posed the question, he waited for someone else to give him reasons for his own violent behavior. No answers were offered by anyone present, and finally, he begged to be shot.

At about seven o'clock that evening, thirty-year-old police officer Sanford Eldredge Kinnecom and another officer, Frank Holden, arrived to take Frank to the East Greenwich County jail, located on King Street. Frank explained to the officers that he had a history of mental problems and believed that he had killed his daughter while under the influence of something beyond his control. Great efforts by him, later joined by the great efforts of his attorney, to rid himself of all responsibility in the murder would begin at this time.

"I could not have struck her if I knew that I was hurting her," he said.

The officers began to pose specific questions to Frank in an attempt to gain some type of understanding concerning his ability to kill his own daughter. They asked him what it was that had caused him to bring Maggie to Rocky Point that day. He stated that he did not know the answer to that question and claimed he had no recollection at all of when he got there or even how he got there.

"I remember going to Attleboro to bring her home," he admitted. But the hours between his departure from Attleboro, Massachusetts, and the fatal blow to his daughter's head were allegedly missing from his memory. It was the sight of his daughter's blood that finally snapped him back into reality, he said.

Authorities sent telegraphs out to Frank's family, informing them of all that had transpired. Frank had been incarcerated. And their little Maggie was dead.

2

THE PARK

The People's Popular Place

Before and after the unspeakable occurrence on August 28, 1893, Rocky Point Amusement Park was one of the country's premier destinations. It was known as the place to go for exciting rides, amazing attractions and the most delicious seafood dinners money could buy.

During the early 1800s, the Warwick, Rhode Island seaside property was merely an untouched portion of the beautiful estate owned by two daughters of Thomas Stafford and Polly Rhodes, who had a total of twelve children. Thomas had purchased the magnificent land with the breathtaking ocean view in 1726. Phebe Smith Stafford, who married Jasper Lyon, and Mary Eliza Stafford, who married Thomas Holden, had inherited the serene property that would eventually be transformed into a nationally famous Rhode Island park.

In the 1840s, it was common for pleasure boats to take passengers sailing down the picturesque Narragansett Bay. Sea captain William Winslow had recently arrived with the *Argo*, a short, wide boat he co-owned with Captains Barton and Drown out of Newark, New Jersey. Winslow ran the boat between Warren and Providence and always marveled at the beauty of the Stafford sisters' land as the boat passed calmly by.

Situated along the shore between Conimicut Point and Warwick Neck Light, the property was a picture of beautiful confusion, appearing as if Mother Nature had simply tossed ledges, caves, plants and bushes into a hasty disarray of enchanting wonder. One summer day, Winslow decided to approach Jasper to ask if his wife and sister-in-law might give him permission to anchor there during his sails so that his passengers could enjoy stepping into the wondrous scene. The sisters consented, and Winslow's first passengers to disembark on the land were a small group of students from Dr. Hall's Sunday school. The following week, he arrived with another class of Sunday school children and 520 members of the Providence First Congregational Church, all ready to enjoy a memorable picnic. He began to make stops there often, sending parties from the *Argo* ashore via smaller boats.

By 1847, Winslow's pleasure sails, with their added attraction, had become so popular that he made arrangements with forty-three-year-old Mary Eliza to buy her half of the eighty-nine-acre estate for $1,200. Not long after, he made the same deal with Phebe and became the new owner of the property in its entirety. Twice a day, he transported passengers from Providence to the new "Winslow's Rocky Point" for just twenty-five cents per person. Admission to the park was free.

While the view was enough to be appreciative of, Winslow wanted to offer his passengers even more enjoyment. In 1852, he added a sea swing to the grounds. A large apparatus, built several feet out into the water, it spun around in a circle to the delight of those seated in its suspended swings. Adding further excitement, a Spanish Fandango roller coaster was also

Summer people opened their cottages just steps away from Rocky Point Park. *Vintage postcard, author's collection.*

erected. Winslow built a wharf that jutted out into the sea so that the *Argo* and other boats carrying passengers bound for Rocky Point were able to sail directly to the park without having to use the smaller boats to get everyone on dry land.

As other parks along the bay were experiencing the same popularity as Winslow's, the owners of other excursion boats desired to sail their passengers to Winslow's wharf as well, where it was convenient for them to walk to the destinations of their choice. Issues concerning the use of the wharf persisted for years. When J.A. Littlefield opened a new resort called Horn Spring just down the bay, its excursion boats began docking at Winslow's wharf, where passengers disembarked and walked the short distance to Horn Spring. Winslow wasn't at all happy about this. Horn Spring had quickly become known as a haven for gambling and intoxication. Its shore dinners were managed by bake master Smith Shaw, and there were many who patronized the resort for its great food. However, it was also popular due to its roulette wheel, large dance hall and free-flowing liquor. Winslow didn't want the likes of such people leaving Horn Spring and venturing back to his family-oriented, sober grounds. He built a high board fence across the beach to keep patrons from other parks off the Rocky Point property. He also built a tall picket fence across

The Shore Dinner Hall at Rocky Point, where patrons begged for the recipe used to make the park's famous clamcakes. *Vintage postcard, courtesy Jules Antiques & General Store.*

the end of the wharf, with a large double gate permitting entrance only to those who were there to visit his park.

For those boat owners not commissioned by Winslow but desiring to deliver passengers to his park, such as the owners of the *Canonicus*, the *New Clifton* and the *Golden Gate*, he charged them a twenty-five-cent landing fee. In 1865, he added another boat, the *Bay Queen*, to the fleet of vessels making their way daily to Rocky Point.

Perhaps the smartest idea the sea captain came up with was that of following the tradition of parks providing seafood dinners. He had a large restaurant constructed on the park grounds that he called the Shore Dinner Hall. His wife, known as "Mother Winslow," cooked all the food, and the menu in 1859 offered a dinner of baked clams, baked potatoes, sweet corn, baked fish, fish chowder and brown bread, all for a grand total of forty cents. It didn't take long for the Rocky Point dining experience to become nationally famous, and people came en masse just for the food alone.

By July 1862, the park had become so busy that Winslow published the following ad in a local newspaper: "On and after July 21, Winslow's Rocky Point will be open for private boarders. Parties intending to visit the above place, expecting accommodations, must first make application to the

Another view of the Shore Dinner Hall at Rocky Point Park. The restaurant would be rebuilt several times over the life of the resort. *Vintage postcard, courtesy Jules Antiques & General Store.*

proprietor. Due notice will be given as soon as arrangements can be made for a boat to make regular trips."

A large residential dormitory for the park's employees called Rock Cottage was built on the grounds, as well as a theater called Forest Circle, which later became known as Forest Casino. The theater provided some of the best minstrel shows and stage performances around, including Buckley's Serenaders, an Ethiopian burlesque opera troupe and a thirteen-piece brass band under the supervision of banjo player and tenor G. Swain Buckley. One of the most popular shows was Duprez & Greene's Minstrels, composed of French Canadian Charles H. Duprez and local theater professional J.A. Greene, who performed their show at the park for many years. Greene later organized J.A. Green's Mocking Bird Minstrels, a group of African American

The circle swing at Rocky Point. *Vintage postcard, courtesy Jules Antiques & General Store.*

men from Pennsylvania. That group also performed at Rocky Point and was later managed by "Big Dick" Melville; however, it was not overly successful. Duprez had begun his employment at the park by running the Fandango. He went on to become one of the most well-known minstrel managers in the country. After forty years of success in his career, he returned to his amusement park roots, taking a job at Crescent Park as a merry-go-round operator.

The Forrest Amazons were another popular act at Rocky Point. Organized by Noah D. Payne, who also went by the name of Frank Forrest, the minstrel group was unique in that it was composed of only women. Payne later went on to publish the *Providence Morning Herald*.

The Four Cohans, a vaudeville family that included the not-yet-famous George Michael Cohan, his parents and his sister, also entertained crowds at the park's theater. Despite the memories of fun and laughter that would be made, it was this building that would serve as Maggie Sheffield's place of death.

A carousel, a bowling alley and other simple amusements were added to Rocky Point, which Winslow intended to be the most sought-after picnicking area in the state. Surrounded by the majestic backdrop of rolling hills, jagged cliffs and the sea, the new park was a sight to behold.

Rocky Point's boat landing, beyond which a fantasyland along the Atlantic Ocean awaited. *Vintage postcard, courtesy Jules Antiques & General Store.*

After enjoying the great success of his venture for nearly twenty years, Winslow sold the park to Byron Sprague in 1865 for $60,000. Sprague was the cousin of millionaire governor William Sprague of Cranston, as well as Amasa Sprague, the county sheriff who would later refuse to sign the petition allowing Frank to undergo a psychological examination at the jailhouse. Sprague had just retired from his position at the family business, A&W Sprague and Company, and spent about $300,000 developing Rocky Point into an unforgettable resort where caterer Hiram Maxfield served up delicious shore dinners. A large, pleasant-looking bearded man who was born on October 20, 1823, Maxfield later opened his own park called Silver Spring along the bay in East Providence. His son later took over that resort. Had Frank's wishes to disembark at Silver Spring been granted that fateful August day many years later, Maggie's murder might have occurred there instead of at Rocky Point.

As a young man, Maxfield had worked as a confectioner. In 1860, he became a sheriff in Providence County. Before and after the Civil War, he kept a hotel and offered "entertainment" in the form of billiard tables and beverages from his retail liquor business, and it was during the war that he became an expert at preparing shore dinners. By the time he opened Silver Spring, he was known as the "king of the shore" for his catering abilities.

Rides such as Rocky Point's circle swing added even more reasons for patrons to visit the premier seaside picnic grounds. *Vintage postcard, courtesy Jules Antiques & General Store.*

Rocky Point's observation tower. *Vintage postcard, courtesy Jules Antiques & General Store.*

The dinner hall at his resort was a spacious building able to seat six hundred people. Cottages were also available for rent on the grounds. The former dealer of intoxicating drinks advertised his park as keeping within strict temperance principles. He died in the summer of 1884, nine years before Maggie's death.

Byron Sprague made many changes in Rocky Point during his ownership. He constructed a ten-floor octagonal observatory, which stood 250 feet above sea level and allowed visitors to climb the stairs to the top and enjoy the breathtaking view for miles. A winding staircase snaked around the structure with landings on each floor and a window situated on all eight sides of every story.

He also added a hotel to the grounds. The massive three-story structure was situated atop a hill overlooking the landing area. It contained three hundred rooms and its own boathouse and livery stable. A large piazza wrapped around the front of the lower story, and the roof was topped with a cupola.

Beside the hotel, Sprague built the large Mansion House, to be used as his personal summer retreat. The top floor was reserved for his home and office while the ground floor housed a café, which served everything from sandwiches to full-course meals. The mansion faced the bay and provided an incredible view of Newport.

Right: The majestic observation tower at Rocky Point provided an incredible view of the bay. *Vintage postcard, Courtesy Jules Antiques & General Store.*

Below: The Mansion House at Rocky Point Park. *Vintage postcard, author's collection.*

The dance hall at Rocky Point. *Vintage postcard, courtesy Jules Antiques & General Store.*

Sprague added another boat, the *City of Newport*, to the park's excursion vessels in 1867. But despite his great investment of time and money, he did not hold on to the property for long. In 1869, he sold the park to the American Steamboat Company, which later changed its name to the Continental Steamboat Company. It owned the *Bay Queen* steamer, which made regular runs to Rocky Point. Improvements and additions to the park went on, to the tune of $200,000.

That year, in July, the Ninth Army Corps and Burnside Expedition held its annual reunion on the park grounds. A clambake was enjoyed, General Ambrose Burnside was reelected as president of the organization and a banquet was attended at the park's luxurious hotel. After a discussion, the group chose Niagara Falls as the location for the next year's reunion.

By the 1870s, Rocky Point had grown to include a host of new amusements, such as a shooting gallery, trained animals, trapeze artists, musicians, dancers and a cage chock-full of monkeys. The hotel, in all its luxurious grandeur, was being run by Louis Harmon Humphrey, a native of Connecticut, and the meals served to its guests were prepared using fresh produce grown on the park's large farm located at the north end of the property.

Regular deliveries of milk and cream were supplied by Benjamin Gorton of Providence, and ice cream was made from scratch right there at the park.

The Ferris wheel thrilled Rocky Point patrons. *Vintage postcard, courtesy Jules Antiques & General Store.*

Day visitors could order strawberry, lemon or vanilla ice cream. Those staying at the hotel had their choice of more exotic flavors.

The bay flowed past an incredibly long stretch of beautiful parks and exciting vacation resorts: Smith's Palace, Mount Hope, Horn Spring, Portsmouth Grove, Oakland Beach and Cherry Grove, to name just a few. Because of this, the Rocky Point wharf continued to be the site of problems for its owners. Steamboats regularly pulled up to it, letting out passengers bound for other parks. No amount of fencing or other deterrents, such as tipping the wharf with iron spikes, seemed to stop such actions. A rival boat eventually rammed into the wharf and demolished it, forcing the construction of a new one. However, a replacement was a necessity. Rocky Point was drawing visitors from all over the country, and Rhode Island was quickly becoming the most popular resort area in all of New England.

The American Steamboat Company soon found itself unable to handle the large flow of visitors and decided to add yet more steamboats to its fleet, including the *Day Star* and the *Crystal Wave*. One of its boats, the *River Belle*, made its last passage to the park on July 4, 1872, with three thousand patrons aboard. By 1874, the steamer *Florence* was also making trips to the resort.

Trains carried passengers to the depot on Canal Street and let them off so that they could walk onto the steamboat wharf on Dyer Street. There, they

The Democrat's Inn, one of the many gathering places at Rocky Point Park. *Vintage postcard, author's collection.*

There was nothing quite like a summer day at the beach and Rocky Point Park. *Vintage postcard, author's collection.*

The chutes slide at Rocky Point. *Vintage postcard, courtesy Jules Antiques & General Store.*

would board whichever boat was headed toward their ultimate destination and begin their sail down Narragansett Bay. After the turn of the century, the railroads would become electrified, and a loop was extended into the grounds of Rocky Point so that patrons could save themselves, through the use of trollies, the chore of walking to the park.

Despite the new thrilling rides and growing variety of amusements, one of the biggest selling points of the park was still the Shore Dinner Hall. Rhode Island had long been world famous for its clambakes, and many felt that there was no place that did it better than Rocky Point. After many bushels of clams had been dug from their security in the warm, wet sand, large pits were dug deep into the ground along the seashore. The pits were filled with wood and lined with rocks before a fire was set inside. Once the wood had been burned and the rocks were smoldering hot, the ashes would be raked out. A piece of wet canvas was laid down over the rocks, and lobsters were laid on top of it. Seaweed soaked in saltwater was placed over the lobsters and each ensuing layer to keep the steam inside the pit. Ears of fresh sweet corn were added next, then potatoes and then clams. At the very top of the pile, another large canvas soaked in seawater was carefully put in place and the meal cooked for several hours.

The clambake was eaten in the exact reverse of how it was placed in the pit. Once the clams opened, they were enjoyed first while giving the corn, potatoes and lobster more time over the heat. Later, after removing

Visitors to Rocky Point Park watch a clambake from behind a protective fence. *Vintage postcard, author's collection.*

the topmost layer of seaweed, the corn and potatoes were taken out and enjoyed, followed by the lobsters. Drawn butter was always on hand, and watermelon or Indian pudding usually provided a final complement to the feast. At Rocky Point, the sea breeze regularly carried the delicious scent of steaming seafood over the grounds as plumes of white smoke drifted upward from the large pits.

The park was once the site of the largest clambake ever held in Rhode Island. In June 1877, when U.S. president Rutherford Hayes came to the park, more than 250 bushels of clams were prepared. Hayes had come to Rhode Island for the purpose of visiting Newport and Providence. While at Rocky Point, he made history by becoming the first president to ever use a telephone. Fred A. Gower, an agent for Alexander Graham Bell, had connected a wire between the park and the City Hotel in Providence, where Bell was staying. Putting the machine to his mouth, Gower told his employer, "Professor Bell, I have the honor to present to you the president of the United States who is listening on the other telephone. Do you understand?" Witnesses in the room watched as Hayes's lips curved up into a smile. He pulled the telephone away from his ear to look down at it. "This is wonderful," he replied.

The call did not last long. Hayes reported that while he was able to hear words over the machine, it was difficult to make out sentences.

The Shore Dinner Hall, packing in the crowds at Rocky Point. *Vintage postcard, courtesy Jules Antiques & General Store.*

Additions to the park continued with the construction of the toboggan ride, operated by Edward Tatro, in 1878, and changes were made to the menu at the Shore Dinner Hall, as well. In 1880, one could enjoy a dinner of clam chowder, baked clams, two kinds of baked fish, white bread, brown bread, corn on the cob, tomatoes and watermelon, all for just fifty cents. For those who wished to add lobster to their meal, they could do so for an additional twenty-five cents. At the Rocky Point Hotel, managed by E.H. Kent, transient guests found quality accommodations for three dollars per day. Those wishing to stay longer paid between ten and fifteen dollars per week, depending on the location of the room.

To Rhode Island's great despair, the hand of fate wasn't kind to its beloved ocean resort on the morning of March 16, 1883, when a fire broke out inside the park's hotel. A fire engine kept in the hotel basement, known as the Little Giant, was brought out and put into service, but the fire raged out of control. None of the park's boats was berthed, and they were therefore unable to bring men and firefighting equipment to the scene. In desperation, the park's manager contacted the owner of a rival boat company to ask for its assistance in extinguishing the blaze.

The company agreed to help and gathered firemen and apparatus to be put aboard the *Canonicus* and transported to Rocky Point. However, the

A bird's-eye view of Rocky Point Park. *Lithograph made by L. Sunderland of Providence in 1878, courtesy of the Library of Congress.*

Rocky Point Park, which began as a serene homestead, would go on to become one of the oldest amusement parks in the country. *Vintage postcard, courtesy Jules Antiques & General Store.*

engine the firemen had secured would not fit aboard the boat, so it was necessary to wait for the return of the *City of Newport* to load that boat with the men and equipment. They arrived too late, however. The flames had already consumed the glorious hotel, the Shore Dinner Hall, the boathouse and many other structures. Within hours, the flawlessly beautiful grounds of Rocky Point were suddenly strewn with ashes and rubble.

Although the other structures were rebuilt, the hotel was not.

The year 1887 brought forth the sad death of one of the park's most beloved figures: Katie, the sarsaparilla-drinking black bear. The tame beast had long been a favorite feature of patrons, as she uncorked bottles of her favorite drink and gulped down the contents.

That August, a mass temperance meeting was held on the park grounds, as speakers attempted to convince the crowd that imbibing alcohol would lead to nothing but personal and collective ruin.

Also that year, the Continental Steamboat Company was sued when a patron was injured on the grounds. During the summer, the Florists Club of Boston had made arrangements for an outing, whereby the steamboat company would transport the group to Rocky Point, provide it with dinner and furnish a room in which the members could carry out their executive duties for the evening.

On July 25, the night before the event, several club members arrived at the park in possession of two horse loads of whiskey, gin, soda and other beverages that they wished to leave at the grounds for the next day's festivities.

The observation tower at Rocky Point stood like a beacon, high above the rides, concessions and acres of amusements. *Vintage postcard, courtesy Jules Antiques & General Store.*

Mr. Mason, the park's manager, objected to that request, explaining that alcohol was not allowed on the grounds. Finally, he relented and told the club members that he would allow them to leave the intoxicants there only if they were put in the room assigned to them and not taken out.

The following day, nearly 250 members of the florists club arrived at the park. The dinner that had been arranged for them was fully prepared, and it was expected the group would head directly to the Shore Dinner Hall. However, the mass went in the opposite direction and headed for the Mansion House, where the alcohol was being stored. As members crossed the piazza that stretched across the front of the building, it collapsed, and one member, Timothy Kelly, fell to the ground, fifteen feet below.

Charging the park owners with negligence and seeking restitution for the personal injuries Kelly received, his lawyer, John Burke, argued that his client had suffered due to an insecure, unsafe and defective structure, made so by a lack of necessary support underneath the hotel's piazza.

The defendants argued that the building was not a hotel and that the piazza was never constructed or intended to hold such a large number of people at one time. The building was, in fact, an office building that housed park superintendent John Brannegan and his family and several seasonal employees, according to the defendants. They explained that they usually made rooms in the building available to members of organizations that were

Rocky Point Park offered hours of fun and scenic delights. *Vintage postcard, courtesy Jules Antiques & General Store.*

visiting the park, where they could retreat to count tickets, write up accounts and complete any other business they needed to tend to concerning their visit. The room that had been assigned to the florists club was not a hotel room at all, they went on, but a nine- by thirteen-foot former storage room.

Regardless of the defendants' explanations and arguments, Timothy Kelly won his case.

Former New York theatrical agent Randall Harrington decided to lease the park, despite the damage contained within, in 1888. After investing much time and money into building the grounds back up to their former glory, Harrington began advertising Rocky Point as "the people's popular place."

He added a large outdoor refreshment garden, which could seat 1,000, to the rear of the park and renovated part of the vegetable garden to be used as a ball field. The grandstand there, which could seat 10,000 people, transformed that area of the resort into a gathering spot for throngs of baseball fans. The largest attendance ever recorded at the ball field was 14,060 people.

The Ferris wheel at Rocky Point Park lifted visitors high enough to look out over Narragansett Bay. *Vintage postcard, courtesy Jules Antiques & General Store.*

There was always an uproar among certain members of the local population concerning the highly popular Sunday baseball games held at Rocky Point. Many thought that the official "day of rest" should be honored as such and not tainted by games of sport. But many more felt that, since most other parks were staunch about refraining from baseball on Sundays, Rocky Point was the place to be.

Other popular attractions in the park were the camera obscura, an optical device that projected images on a screen, and a giant waterslide, added in 1892, called the Big Toboggan. Also added was a sixty-foot wooden Ferris wheel designed by Charles Looff, one of the world's most famous builders of carousels. The sixteen chariots each held two passengers, giving them an unforgettable view of the bay from the top of the ride.

There was barely enough time in one day for families to take in all that Rocky Point had to offer, and few left without stopping at the photo studio in the midway to have their portraits taken by photographer Edward Tatro, the former operator of the Big Toboggan ride. Patrons could choose an artificial backdrop from the entertaining selections offered.

Rocky Point opened each year on the first week of July and stayed open until the first week of September. It was ready to welcome guests for business each morning at half past eight and closed its gates at six o'clock at night. Several hours were then spent cleaning the grounds. Alcoholic beverages were still banned on the property, and Sundays found the park closed except for baseball.

Rocky Point's drinking fountain. *Vintage postcard, courtesy Jules Antiques & General Store.*

Many different groups and organizations around New England and beyond held fundraisers, parties and annual outings at Rocky Point. Such was the case when the Fall River Police Department scheduled a fun vacation day for its officers on August 4, 1892. While the law enforcers were enjoying a carefree time, Lizzie Borden's father and stepmother were being savagely murdered back in Fall River. Exactly one year and two weeks later, it was Maggie Sheffield being bludgeoned, right there on the grounds of the park.

3

THE FAMILY

A Wife Immaculate

Frank Howard Sheffield was born in Woodstock, Connecticut, on August 9, 1850. His mother, Charlotte Delana (Howard), was a homemaker, and his father, John Franklin Sheffield, was a Methodist preacher.

The family moved around quite often, answering the call of Reverend Sheffield's chosen career wherever it came from. In 1860, the family resided in Enfield, Connecticut. Ten years later, they were in East Greenwich, Rhode Island. By 1880, they had moved to Cumberland, Rhode Island.

Frank grew up listening intently to his father's powerful sermons about the fundamental aspects of being graceful in the eyes of God. The Methodists did not believe that one was saved by merely doing good deeds but by the strongest faith in the Lord. Redemption would come, preached John, and all who believed in the Lord would be awarded it, even if they had not been able to shun evil or avoid committing wicked deeds while here on earth.

For a time, Frank himself considered going into the ministry and even began studies in the field. However, he changed his mind before becoming ordained and never revisited that righteous path again.

Ironically, considering the shocking events that would come to pass in the future, Frank and his siblings, Mary Charlotte and Charles, would spend time living in a house that neighbored the East Greenwich County jail. In that town, their father served as pastor of the East Greenwich Methodist Church.

Frank's mother died on February 2, 1875, at the age of fifty-two, and his father later married Mary Segur. All three of John and Charlotte's children grew up to become schoolteachers, and in the mid-1870s, Frank took on the position of principal at East Greenwich School.

On December 15, 1876, Frank married Miss Mary Ann Hill of Mystic, Connecticut. Mary's father, Mason Crary Hill, was a master shipbuilder, well known for designing and building the clipper ship *Alboni*. Launched in 1852, the vessel was named after the Italian opera singer Marietta Alboni and carried a figurehead of a dove with an orange branch in its beak. Weighing 917 tons and measuring 156 feet in length, the ship was originally commissioned for trade voyages to Cape Horn. Its worth at the time was over $50,000.

Frank's new father-in-law was well respected and much acquainted with a life of prestige and wealth. However, he had also known the pain of loss and great personal tragedy. His first wife, Mary Ann Williams, was accidentally drowned at the age of twenty-eight when a boat on which she was a passenger overturned on the Mystic River on the Fourth of July 1853. His love for her was evident by the mournful etching he had placed on her gravestone, which reads, "A wife immaculate."

Mason next married Miss Margaret Wheeler. The couple had many children together, including Mary Ann, who was named after her father's first wife.

After Frank and Mary Ann were united in marriage, they took up residence next door to her parents on Greenmanville Avenue in Mystic. On January 11, 1880, Mary Ann gave birth to a dark-haired, blue-eyed baby boy, whom they named Mason Howard Sheffield.

Later that year, the couple moved to Pawcatuck, Connecticut, a small village in the town of Stonington, where they rented a segment of the three-family tenement house at 24 Liberty Street. No immediate relation, the owner of the tenement house was sixty-five-year-old patternmaker and former ship's carpenter Amos Thompson Sheffield, who resided with his own family at 27 Liberty Street.

Frank obtained a job as principal of the recently built Palmer Street School in Pawcatuck. While employed in that position, he was engaged in a freak accident that resulted in an apparent long-standing injury. As he was in the process of ringing the large school bell, the bell somehow maneuvered itself to strike Frank violently on the head. According to all who knew him, this accident caused Frank to have severe headaches on a regular basis for years afterward.

Mary Ann gave birth to the couple's second child, Maggie Segur Sheffield—the middle name perhaps honoring Frank's stepmother—on

The birth certificate of Maggie Segur Sheffield. *Courtesy of Stonington Town Hall.*

January 31, 1888. However, her daughter's entrance into the world would bring about her own demise. On February 7, 1888, just one week after Maggie's birth, Mary Ann died at the age of thirty-three. On the day prior to her death, it became clear to those around her that Mary Ann was not recovering from the birth very well. The painful effects of peritonitis, a condition caused by a hemorrhage of the membranes in the lining of the pelvic wall following the baby's arrival, were setting in.

The inflammation in Mary Ann's abdomen became so severe that it caused her lungs to swell. Already in immense pain, she struggled to breathe, which was at first difficult and then impossible. Frank lost the wife he loved, and Maggie lost the mother she would never know. Mary Ann was buried in the large Elm Grove Cemetery, located right down the road from her parents' house.

Out of nowhere, Frank was faced with a future he had never even imagined. Suddenly, he had become a widower with two small children to raise on his own. He decided to let Mary Ann's parents take Mason into their care. As for his newborn daughter, she would go to live with Frank's parents at their own Danielsonville, Connecticut home. He would remain, alone, at the 24 Liberty Street house.

BUREAU OF VITAL STATISTICS.　　　State of Connecticut.

CERTIFICATE OF DEATH.

To be returned to the Registrar of the Town in which the Death occurred, as the Law directs.

I CERTIFY the following return to be correct from the best information which I can obtain:

*That _her_ name in full was _Mary A Sheffield_

Maiden Name, if wife or widow _Mary A Hill_

Place of Death, No. _24 Liberty_ Street, Town _Pawcatuck_

Number of Families, if tenement house _3_, Duration of Disease _24 hours_

Date of Death _Feb 7_, Residence at time of Death _24 Liberty St_

Sex _Female_, Color _White_, †Race _Cauc_, Occupation _House_

Age _32_ Years, _____ Months, _____ Days.

‡Condition _M_, if a wife or widow, Husband's Name _Frank H Sheffield_

Birthplace _East Woodstock_ Town _Conn_, State or Country.

Father's Name _Marcy C Hill_, Mother's Name _Margaret Hill_

Birthplace of Father _Plainville Ct_, Mother _Lee, Mass._

Cause of Death, { Primary _Uderia Lungs_
　　　　　　　{ Secondary _Puerper Peritonitis_

Signature of Physician, _Edwin R Lewis M D_

Dated at _Westerly_ this _7_ day of _February_ 188_8_

*Insert his or her.
†If other than white— (A.) African, (M.) Mulatto, (I.) Indian. If other races, specify what.
‡Single, Married, or Widowed.
[BE VERY PARTICULAR TO FILL ALL BLANKS.]

Above: The death certificate of Mary Ann Sheffield, who died shortly after giving birth to Maggie. *Courtesy of Stonington Town Hall.*

Right: The grave of Mary Ann Sheffield at Elm Gove Cemetery in Mystic, Connecticut. *Photograph by Kelly Sullivan Pezza.*

The year after Mary Ann's death, Frank resigned from his position at Palmer Street School, believing that making some changes in his life would do him good. He took a new position as principal of Liberty Street School, which stood very near to his residence. However, later that year, he contracted erysipelas, a bacterial infection, and began to feel unwell on a regular basis. His employment was terminated in 1890. By that time, he was married again.

On November 27, 1889, Frank had exchanged vows with Nancy Armeda Sheffield, the thirty-seven-year-old daughter of his former landlord, who had passed away eleven months earlier. A professional dressmaker by trade, Nancy knew the mournful feeling of loss that her new husband surely carried with him. She had already lost four sisters, as well as her mother and now her father.

Frank moved into the 27 Liberty Street house with Nancy and secured a position as a clerk in the freight department of the New York, Providence & Boston Railroad's depot in Westerly, Rhode Island. However, his poor health continued to plague him, and he was soon let go from his employment there due to the fact that he could not perform his job efficiently.

On October 14, 1890, Nancy gave birth to the couple's first child, whom they named Sarah Elizabeth Sheffield. Frank began working for W.D. Sheffield of New Haven as a rent collector, and it might have appeared to some that he had started life anew. But for Frank, it was not that easy to push the past behind and look toward an untainted future.

Those who knew him best could clearly see that something was wrong. All that had been instilled in him by his religious father seemed to have drained away. He wanted nothing to do with religion any longer and refused to even speak about Christianity with anyone unless it was in the form of an argument in which he could try to fray the beliefs of those who were followers.

Frank showed a growing interest in agnosticism and spent time studying the science of its ambivalence. His father was shocked and hurt by the transition his son had made and later, after Maggie's murder, claimed that because Frank had absolutely no reason to commit such a crime, the killing had obviously been the work of a demon.

Despite his ongoing dismissal of deep religious beliefs, Frank would appear at a Methodist meeting a few weeks before that fateful day at Rocky Point and surprise everyone by standing up and asking for their prayers.

What was truly going through Frank Sheffield's mind in those years that followed his wife's untimely death no one close to him seemed to know.

Perhaps he needed an explanation that Christian beliefs did not provide or a soft place to fall when such an answer wasn't available. Perhaps he needed to blame someone for his loss. The small child who would have her young life bludgeoned out of her as a result of Frank's despair had been the ultimate cause of Mary Ann's death. Maggie's existence had replaced that of her mother. Frank possibly wrestled with that thought amid the confusion in his mind.

Nancy may or may not have realized, or accepted, that something was dreadfully wrong with the man she had married. Regardless, on August 2, 1892, she went on to give birth to the second of their children, a son whom they named Amos Thompson Sheffield, after Nancy's father. However, little Amos would never get the opportunity to know his father. The boy had just celebrated his first birthday when Frank committed the unspeakable act that would cause him to be locked away for life.

4

THE ABDUCTION

Why Are You Looking at Me Like That?

On the pleasant Sunday morning of August 27, 1893, Frank Sheffield rose from his bed at seven o'clock. After getting changed into his daytime clothes, he informed Nancy that he needed to make some purchases and was going to take a walk down to Richmond Brother's Grocery, which was located on West Broad Street, not far from their home. Nancy thought whatever errand he was on could wait until later. She had already begun cooking their morning meal. "Breakfast will be ready soon," she told him. But Frank ignored the announcement and continued on with the plans he had made.

After walking out the door, he started down the road. Wherever he went and whatever he did immediately after that no one knew. But he failed to return home when he was done, leaving a cold breakfast and a wondering wife.

Eventually, he made his way to the train depot on Railroad Avenue, where he had been working several months earlier. Approaching the ticket booth, he handed over the fare for transportation to Providence. A man who was standing nearby recognized him.

"Where are you going?" the man asked.

"I'm going to Attleboro to get my child," Frank replied. Despite the fact that his wife was waiting at home with no idea where he was, when the 8:18 a.m. train for the city left, Frank was on it.

Several hours later, when he still hadn't returned home, Nancy became worried and went out looking for him. She had a good reason to be concerned. Frank had been seeing a doctor who had informed Nancy that her husband was not well and that she should take care not to let him wander off alone.

With growing concern, Nancy enlisted the help of Frank's friend twenty-seven-year-old Dennison Hinckley of Westerly. Hinckley was an undertaker and part owner of Hinckley & Mitchell, a furniture store and undertaking business located at 44 High Street in Westerly. He and Frank were both members of Pawcatuck Lodge #90 and had been good friends for quite some time.

Nancy also decided it was a useful idea to send telegrams to Frank's family members, including his sister in Attleboro, to determine whether they had seen him or had any idea of his whereabouts. Unfortunately, the message was not received by Mary Charlotte until the following day.

Frank's sister and her husband, Methodist minister George Edgar Brightman, had been entertaining house guests for the past ten days. Her father and stepmother had come to stay with them for a short time, and since Maggie lived with her paternal grandfather, she was staying there also.

Mary Charlotte was very surprised to see Frank show up on her doorstep at twelve o'clock that afternoon. When she questioned him about his visit, he informed her that he was there to pick up Maggie and take her with him.

Greatly alarmed by his ruffled appearance and fully aware of his recent mental deterioration, Mary Charlotte urged Frank to lie down and take a nap. She explained to him that he would feel much better after he had some sleep. Frank showed little patience with the delay in obtaining custody of his daughter and quickly declined her offer. He acted much too eager, much too desperate, to collect the child and be on his way.

George Brightman returned home from preaching the morning service at the Methodist church to witness his disheveled brother-in-law being adamant about leaving with Maggie. The fidgety way he behaved while arguing with George and his wife, coupled with the strange way he continuously stared at Maggie, made them very uncomfortable.

Even the little girl could see that something was very wrong with her father and the way his eyes were set upon her. "Why are you looking at me like that?" she questioned him.

George desperately tried to reason with Frank. He attempted to convince him that it truly was in his best interest to go in another room and try to get some rest before starting back out for home. Whether he was mentally or physically exhausted by that time, Frank finally relented and went into one of the other rooms, where he slept for several hours.

George immediately sent a telegram to Nancy in order to let her know that Frank was there and safe for the time being. But that message was also delayed until the following day.

When Frank finally awoke later that evening, he joined the rest of the family at the dinner table and partook of a fairly large meal. He was persuaded to remain there at the Brightman house for the rest of the night, as they all believed that Nancy knew of his location via their telegram.

The next morning, when Mary Charlotte received the belated message Nancy had sent her asking if she knew where Frank was, she was wrought with confusion. She took her father and stepmother aside and shared the message with them, as they all tried to figure out why Nancy would send such a telegram when they had already informed her of the situation.

As the three of them spoke privately, Frank quietly took hold of his daughter and walked away from the house.

George had been away from home conducting a funeral service at the time of Frank's departure, and when he returned home, Mary Charlotte alerted him that Frank had disappeared and taken Maggie with him. Other family members were made aware of what had happened, and a search for them was quickly begun.

After the search party had gone out into the town and questioned several people, it was discovered that Frank and his little girl had left North Attleboro on the trolley, heading toward Pawtucket. Pawtucket police were notified to be on the lookout for him, and Nancy was contacted and informed of all that was going on.

By noontime, Frank and Maggie had arrived in Providence, where he purchased tickets for the one o'clock departure of the *Bay Queen* steamer. Once aboard, Frank apparently felt the pangs of hunger again, as he stepped up to the purser and informed him that he desired to stop at Silver Spring to get a shore dinner.

Silver Spring was one of the many summer resort parks situated along Narragansett Bay. Standing within the town of East Providence, it had been opened in 1869 by Hiram Drowne Maxfield, a former caterer at Rocky Point. However, Frank was out of luck. The purser explained to him that this particular boat did not stop at Silver Spring. Its only destinations were Rocky Point Park and Crescent Park. Other passengers on the boat would later relate how their attention had been drawn to Frank's scruffy appearance, strange vacant staring spells and aimless, unusual bodily movements.

With Maggie in tow, Frank got off the boat at Rocky Point and reached into his pocket to retrieve the ten-cent fare. They went directly to the park's

Silver Spring, where Frank Sheffield had planned to enjoy a shore dinner on the day he killed his daughter. *Vintage postcard, author's collection.*

Rocky Point's Shore Dinner Hall, famous for its seafood and clambakes. *Vintage postcard, courtesy Jules Antiques & General Store.*

Shore Dinner Hall so that Frank could partake of the near-famous clam cakes, chowder, lobster and fish.

The waiters and ticket-takers at the hall immediately noticed that something was not quite right about Frank's behavior and would later testify that, as Maggie talked incessantly, it was obvious that Frank was trying very hard to pay attention to her but that his gaze was pulled around the room without reason, stopping regularly to stare into nothingness.

He consumed another rather large meal before leaving the dining hall with his daughter and heading up over the hill that led toward the theater and the high cliffs jutting up around the edge of the park.

The time was about half past three. In less than an hour, the happy little girl walking alongside her father, taking in the gay laughter and barrel organ melodies that surrounded her, would be dead.

5

THE ARREST

I Can't Remember of Killing but One

Seventy-year-old Warwick medical examiner Moses Fifield of Centerville, Rhode Island, performed the autopsy on Maggie's body at about nine o'clock that evening. He later stated in his report that there was a compound comminuted fracture of the skull above the right side of the forehead, as well as another fracture, about six inches long, across the top of the head. He added that, as a result of the injury, the little girl's brain was protruding through the top of the head.

George Brightman had been in attendance at a Methodist meeting that evening when a newspaper reporter arrived there to speak with him. The reporter informed George that there had been a terrible tragedy at Rocky Point Park. He set out for home, returning at about ten o'clock to receive a message that the telegraph company had failed to deliver two and a half hours earlier. Reading the message, he was finally to learn that his young niece had been killed and his brother-in-law had been arrested. Now someone had to go claim Maggie's body. The little girl had been transported to the undertaking rooms of thirty-seven-year-old Thomas Francis Monahan, located on Wickenden Street in Providence. George arrived there sometime around midnight. While the body of his dead child was being probed, Frank had become strangely silent in his jail cell, miles away.

Early the next morning, authorities called in Frank's former in-laws for an interview. Mason and Margaret Hill told them that they had recently received three postal cards from Frank informing them that he was in Attleboro and

RETURN OF A DEATH.

CITY OF PROVIDENCE.

1. Date of Death? *Aug 28* 189*3*.
2. Name in Full? *Margie Segar Sheffield*
3. Age? *5* Years *6* Months *28* Days.
4. Place of Death, Street and Number? *Rocky Point* Ward
5. Usual Residence? *Davisonville Conn*
6. Sex? *Female* 7. Color? *W*
8. Single, Married, Widowed, or Divorced?
9. Husband's Name?
10. Occupation?
11. Birthplace? State or Country *Stonington* City *Conn*
12. Father's Name? *Frank H Sheffield*
13. Mother's Name? *Hill*
14. Parents' Birthplaces? Fa. Mo. *Conn*
15. Where to be Buried? *Mystic Conn.*
Davisonville Hucky, Informant.

PHYSICIAN'S CERTIFICATE.

Please state different causes of death in order of occurrence as FULLY as possible, particularly in DOUBTFUL cases.

Date of Death? *Aug 28* 189*5*. Hour? M.
Name? *Margie Sheffield*
Causes of Death? *Compound Comminuted Fracture of the Skull*

Duration of Disease? Primary _____ Secondary _____

M Fifield, M.D. PHYSICIAN.
Medical Examiner

I certify that the above is a true return to the best of my knowledge and belief.

T. H. Munahan UNDERTAKER.

The death certificate of Maggie Segur Sheffield, who died from a compound fracture of the skull, caused by her father, Frank. *Courtesy Warwick Town Hall.*

was in good health. After receiving the message that he had gone missing and taken Maggie with him, they were very concerned, they said.

The Hills had thought there was something wrong with Frank for quite some time, the couple shared, ever since the first time he had aimlessly wandered away from home and showed up on their doorstep. Frank's problems, they surmised, had resulted from him overworking himself at the railroad freight depot in Westerly.

When they were questioned concerning what they knew about Frank receiving a blow to the head from a school bell, the Hills said they knew about the incident and that it had caused him to experience frequent and severe headaches.

They stated that they were not aware of any serious mental issues Frank might have been dealing with, as they saw him only occasionally. They claimed that Frank had loved his daughter very much, favored her even, and that they had never had cause to worry that he might do something to harm her.

It was not only Frank but everyone who favored Maggie, Mason confessed. "She was the sweetest little thing you ever saw."

Later that morning, forty-nine-year-old coroner Albert Rowland Greene of Apponaug arrived at the Fourth District Court's office of the clerk with a warrant sworn out by Justice of the Peace Charles C. Phelps of Apponaug. Greene handed the warrant to the deputy sheriff, forty-nine-year-old Michael Bernard Lynch of Warwick, so that it could be served to Frank.

At 9:30 a.m., Dennison Hinckley and fifty-one-year-old court clerk and former cigar-maker Thomas James Tilley accompanied Lynch to the jailhouse, where Frank had been brought and incarcerated the previous evening.

The men made their way down a corridor to the cell where the prisoner was secured and found him half reclined on his cot, his head on a pillow and his eyes staring into space. Lynch prepared to inform him that he was about to be formally charged with murder.

"Good morning, Mr. Sheffield," Lynch offered. Frank looked over at him.

"Would you please get up?" Lynch asked.

Frank did as he was asked and left the cell to follow the men into another room.

There, jail keeper Mrs. Smith, Tilley and the others waited while Frank seated himself in a nearby rocking chair. He listened with concentrated interest as the warrant, which charged him with willfully, maliciously and feloniously assaulting and killing his daughter, was read to him by Lynch.

"You have heard the warrant read, charging you with the murder of your daughter Maggie, alias Eliza Roe," Tilley said. "What do you say to the charge? Are you guilty or not guilty?"

Frank thought hard, narrowing his eyes as if in the process of deep recollection. But the answer to that question was not forthcoming.

"Are you guilty or not guilty?" Tilley asked.

When Frank finally spoke, his voice was quiet and dripping with despair. "I killed my little girl," he said.

Hinckley attempted to comfort Frank, but for several moments, Frank said nothing and just stared at Hinckley as if he were a complete stranger. Then he extended his hand and replied, "Oh, yes. This is Mr. Hinckley."

"Did you sleep well last night?" Hinckley asked.

"I don't know," Frank answered. Those employed at the jailhouse had noticed just before midnight that Frank's short intervals of sleep were interrupted by something that seemed to be causing him physical pain.

Frank immediately became very agitated. "I must go to Mystic today to see my boy," he announced.

Hinckley, as well as the others in the room, knew that the man before them was not going to Mystic or anywhere else.

"What does Eliza Roe mean?" Frank suddenly asked them.

The men explained to him that the name was simply an alias. It had been used as a reference to Maggie until they were able to determine her real identity.

Just hours after Frank was charged with murder, his daughter's remains were transported from Providence to Westerly, where they arrived at five o'clock that evening. There, the body was prepared by Hinckley for the next day's funeral.

Almost immediately after Maggie's body arrived in town, Nancy sent a telegram to her husband, telling him she would be coming to visit him at the jail later in the day. Before her arrival, seventy-six-year-old Reverend Smith Bartlett Goodenow of the First Congregational Church, which Nancy attended, stopped by to see Frank. The two men reminisced for a good amount of time about happy occasions that had taken place during their friendship. But eventually, the conversation turned to the events of the afternoon of August 28.

"I can remember being with Maggie among the rocks at Rocky Point," Frank recalled. He said he believed there were other people nearby the cliffs as he and Maggie happily conversed.

"The last thing I recall is Maggie asking me for my handkerchief, so that she could tie it into the form of a doll," he said. He didn't remember what happened after that. His next conscious memory, he claimed, was the look in Maggie's eyes as she stared up at him with blood gushing from her head.

"I don't remember picking up the stone or striking her with it," he told the reverend. He then strangely added, "They charge me with murdering two girls, but I can't remember of killing but one and that was my little Maggie."

Frank had apparently been very confused by his earlier conversation with the police officers. He had somehow come to believe that "Eliza Roe" was another child who had been killed, even though it had been thoroughly explained to him that the name was merely an alias.

Frank then informed the reverend that he was expecting a visit from his wife and was very concerned for her safety. He requested of the jail matron that she not let him out of his cell while Nancy was there. He explained that

The grave of Maggie Segur Sheffield at Elm Gove Cemetery in Mystic, Connecticut. *Photograph by Kelly Sullivan Pezza.*

he was afraid he might go violently insane again and end up harming his wife this time.

Later that day, Frank received another visitor in the form of a man identified as Officer Gavitt.

"Do you know me?" Gavitt asked, as he entered Frank's cell.

"Yes," Frank answered. "You come from Westerly. I have seen you often around the railroad station."

"How are you feeling?" Gavitt asked.

"I have terrible pains in my head," Frank replied. He told Gavitt that he knew he was in a really bad situation.

On Wednesday afternoon at half past one, Maggie was laid out in her father's home on Liberty Street as her uncle George preached the funeral sermon with the assistance of Reverend Goodenow. The service was a simple one, consisting of only one hymn, a prayer and some brief remarks. Her body was then taken to Elm Grove Cemetery, and she was placed in the ground beside her mother.

6

THE HEARING

He Might Have Brought It upon Himself

A preliminary hearing was held on September 5, 1893, at the Kent County courthouse on Main Street in East Greenwich. The defendant entered the courtroom wearing a somber black suit and a matching cap, which was pulled tightly over his head. With him was Nathan Barber Lewis, whom he had employed to act as his attorney.

Lewis was a fifty-one-year-old native of Exeter, Rhode Island. After having been elected to the legislature in 1886, he was chosen to preside over the Second Judicial Court District of Rhode Island. A widower who had lost all but one of his four children in infancy, Lewis had been a private in the Rhode Island Seventh Regiment during the Civil War. He was well respected and staunch in his belief that Frank was insane at the time of the murder. He confidently entered his client's plea of not guilty.

Under the law, a person must possess evil intent during the committal of a crime in order to be found guilty of such a crime. The law also states that when a person with a diseased or defective mind commits a crime, he or she has no capacity to know the quality of his or her actions and can therefore not be held responsible. It was the belief of Lewis that Frank was incapable of forming the intent to commit murder or realize what he was doing when he killed his daughter.

While the attorney made his explanations to the court, Frank sat in his chair silently, alternating between looking terribly bored and covering his face with his hands. Once Lewis was finished stating his case, the prosecuting attorney, Albert Rowland Greene, who was also the coroner, took over everyone's attention.

Kent County courthouse, where Frank Sheffield stood trial for killing his daughter. *Vintage postcard, author's collection.*

At the time forty-nine years old, Greene had graduated from Brown University, Cornell University and the Michigan University School of Law. Also a veteran of the Civil War, he had been president and a member of the Warwick Town Council for three years. Another well-respected citizen and lawyer, he was confident in the guilt of the man before him.

In front of the court, Greene displayed a brown paper bag from which he carefully removed a little girl's dress and shoes, both darkly stained with blood. He called Officer Kinnecom to the stand and asked the policeman if he could identify the articles of clothing. As Kinnecom testified that they were the clothes Maggie had been wearing at the time of the murder, Frank removed his hands from his face and looked up at the evidence. He then pulled his gaze away and lowered his chin to his chest.

No defense was offered at the preliminary hearing, but Judge Warner pronounced Frank probably guilty and set the matter down for trial. While he was being led from the courtroom to return to his cell at the jail, Frank's calmness disappeared and he exploded in a severe bout of emotion. Physical restraint was necessary to subdue him, and this made Lewis even more determined to prove that his client was insane.

The following day, Lewis paid a visit to fifty-seven-year-old Judge Pardon Elisha Tillinghast and asked him to order a psychological examination of Frank. Tillinghast stated that he would do so only if a petition calling for such an examination was presented to him giving him jurisdiction. Lewis immediately prepared the proper petition and went to see fifty-five-year-old Deputy Sheriff Amasa Sprague in order to get his signature.

Expecting that Lewis would soon return with the signed petition, Tillinghast contacted a Providence doctor, asking him to go to the jail and complete a thorough examination of Frank.

However, upon Lewis's request for a signature, Sprague decided to consult the attorney general first regarding his personal opinion on an examination of the prisoner. Lewis's ability to do anything further was delayed for several days until Sprague contacted him to say he had decided not to sign the document.

Sprague's position could not be altered, so Lewis visited the Office of the Rhode Island Agent of Charities and Corrections to appeal for help. There, he was informed that the officer he would need to speak with had left on a trip to see the World's Fair, and nothing could be undertaken until he came back.

Eventually, the officer returned and met with Lewis, explaining to him that if Deputy Sprague felt Frank could be cared for properly at the jail and was not suffering from his incarceration there, then he did not feel the need to arrange a transferal. Lewis pointed out that the petition was not a request to have Frank moved but merely to have him examined so that a professional determination could be made regarding his sanity or lack of it. If such an examination indicated that Frank *was* suffering from insanity, Lewis added, it would still have to be proven before the judge would order him moved to a hospital.

If indications of insanity were discovered and subsequently proven, Frank would leave the confines of the jail cell and be transported to a psychiatric hospital. The officer informed Lewis that he didn't think Frank could be tried if he were admitted to the hospital, and therefore, it was best that he remain in jail. Upset by such a rationalization, Lewis asked him why the state would *want* to try an insane man who is not legally responsible for his own acts.

Perhaps, the officer suggested, the situation was not as simple as that. "He might have brought it upon himself," he argued. After all, there were reports swirling around town from reputable sources that Frank had been a regular user of cocaine for at least the last five years, while others claimed it was opium he was using.

7

THE DRUG RUMOR

On Coca

B y 1886, opium had become as common to Americans as apple pie. The dark brown gummy substance was sold in pure form right over any pharmacy's counter. More commonly, it was used as an ingredient in many familiar medications of the time. Everything from cough syrups for children to adult headache relievers listed opium as an element in the mixture.

Opium cases, containing all people needed to inject themselves into oblivion, were also sold over the counter, as plain or ornate as one wished to get. The cases could be engraved with the user's name and contained a needle, syringe and small vessels in which to keep the drug.

In addition to injecting opium, one could also smoke it, as was obvious from the number of opium dens that had popped up all over America by that time. Many thought that Frank Sheffield was quite likely to be an opium user, as the rumors indicated. Several signs of opium use *did* seem to be apparent in the behavior he regularly exhibited.

Opium causes one to experience headaches and a ringing in the ears, not unlike the symptoms Frank suffered from, which he attributed to being clanged in the head by the school bell. It causes objects and people to appear faded and distorted, which would explain why Frank had a habit of staring so strangely at things around him. Under the influence of opium, sounds and words are not heard clearly, and this would explain Frank's delayed response whenever anyone asked him a question. And opium makes the user restless and inclined to wander aimlessly for extended and exhaustive periods of time, which would easily explain the occasions on which Frank wandered away from home. In addition, the drug has a tendency to cause severe memory loss.

However, opium has several other side effects that did not correspond at all with Frank's behavior. Its use has been shown to bring on a calm, comfortable, serene feeling. As the user begins to feel more self-assured, worries drift away, and a kind, understanding patience sets in. It would, in fact, be out of character for a person under the influence of opium to just suddenly kill someone.

Others did not believe Frank was an opium user. That was not the only rumor going around about his strange and long-standing mental condition. Some people who knew him were claiming he was constantly resorting to the use of cocaine, starting from just before or just after the time of his wife's death.

Again, several effects of this drug could easily explain Frank's behavior. Cocaine causes the user to experience increased oxygen intake, which brings about a strange kind of talkativeness and a very high level of energy. But just as the opium addiction theory didn't exactly match Frank's profile, neither did the theory of cocaine addiction. Frank talked of being hungry and eager to obtain a meal while riding the *Bay Queen* to Rocky Point. He ate a large meal when he arrived at the dinner hall and had eaten a large meal at his sister's house the night before. While opium tends to make a person very hungry, cocaine nearly erases the appetite, causing users to go for days without eating.

Like opium, cocaine was sold over the counter at pharmacies, both in pure form and as an ingredient in medicines for babies, children and adults. In 1886, it even became the main ingredient in a new soft drink that soared in popularity. Cocaine was almost revered for its miraculous power, and psychologist Sigmund Freud highly recommended its use after utilizing himself as a guinea pig and performing several experiments with the drug. In 1884, he published *On Coca* and began touting cocaine as a sure cure for opium addiction.

Perhaps Frank was using opium. Perhaps he was using cocaine, too. It's possible he was using one drug to cease his reliance on the other. Or maybe he wasn't using any drugs at all. There were still those who believed that Frank was simply out of his mind through no fault of his own.

8

THE TRIAL

I Don't Think the Man Is Crazy

O n October 9, 1893, the *State of Rhode Island v. Frank H. Sheffield* on the charge of murder came to fruition.

Thirty-four-year-old Coventry constable James B. Fish had picked up the prisoner from the jailhouse that morning and brought him in for trial. Frank entered the courtroom neatly clad in a Prince Albert coat over a black suit. Everyone noticed that his usually close-cut beard had grown nearly two inches in length since the murder. However, the beard did little to conceal the look of utter despair on his face.

He was brought to the seat between that of his attorney, Nathan Lewis, and that of his brother-in-law, George Brightman. The courtroom was packed with witnesses and spectators, and as more people continued to file in, they found that there was standing room only.

The jury included no women, no mothers of little girls who would have felt sickened by the nightmarish act that had taken place that terrible day at Rocky Point. Instead, a panel of mostly middle-aged male farmers was selected to decide the fate of the man before them.

Selected as jury foreman was forty-eight-year-old Fenner Kent, a farmer from Coventry. Also serving on the panel were William H. Brown, fifty years old and also a farmer from Coventry; Atmore Robinson Brown, age forty-five, a West Greenwich farmer; fifty-seven-year-old Ichabod Fish, another farmer from West Greenwich; George A. Carr, a twenty-seven-year-old farmer from Coventry; Wanton Lillibridge Albro, a forty-nine-year-old team driver from West Greenwich; fifty-two-year-old stable

A sketch of Frank Sheffield. *Drawn by Joseph Roland Sullivan.*

owner Joshua Clarke Arnold from East Greenwich; Lafayette Blanchard, age forty-two, a carpenter from Coventry; Byron Killon, a thirty-three-year-old from Coventry; and Warwick resident Frank Oscar Johnson.

Of the jury members selected, two of them stated that they knew absolutely nothing about the case, although it had been front-page news.

Frank H. Gardiner, a thirty-four-year-old teamster from Warwick, was excused from the jury pool when he admitted that he did indeed know about the case and had been reading about it in the local newspapers. He stated that he had already formed an opinion on the guilt of Frank Sheffield.

John B. Gendron of Warwick was also excused, as he was employed by the town as a constable, making him an unsuitable juror.

West Greenwich resident Frank H. Capwell was not accepted to the jury when it was discovered that he was only twenty-two years of age, which was too young to serve.

Charles H. Battey from Coventry, a fifty-one-year-old farmer, also admitted that he had been reading all about the case in the local newspapers, and his opinion on whether Frank was guilty of murder had already been formed. He stated that he couldn't honestly say whether any evidence presented during the trail would alter his opinion. He was thereby excused from jury duty as well.

Also excused was Swedish-born August Abramson, who did not understand the English language well enough to fill the position efficiently.

When Frank's wife, Nancy, entered the courtroom at fifteen minutes past eleven, he made no acknowledgement of her presence. Dressed appropriately in refined mourning clothes, she appeared to be quite nervous. The indictment charging her husband with murder was read, and the defendant entered a plea of not guilty.

Thirty-five-year-old Attorney General Willard Brooks Tanner opened for the State of Rhode Island by describing for the jury what had transpired on the day of the murder. Moses Fifield was the first witness called to the stand. After raising his right hand and swearing to tell the truth, he described in detail the nature of the wounds on Maggie's head.

Robert Quinn, the teenaged house painter who had accompanied Harrington to the murder scene, was called to the stand next. He stated that he had been at Rocky Point Park on the afternoon of August 28 and first saw Maggie at about quarter past four. He said she was lying in the woods near the park, and he believed her to be dead. Quinn described picking up the little dying girl off the ground and carrying her into the park's theater.

Michael Lynch testified in regards to the conversation he'd had with Frank at the county jail at the time the warrant was served.

Newell Belcher and Frank Holden told the jury what they had seen of Frank's behavior that fateful day, as did two employees of the Shore Dinner Hall who described the way Frank oddly stared at the ceiling and occasionally gawked around in a strange manner instead of focusing his attention on his little daughter as she chatted away excitedly.

Tanner closed the state's case that morning at forty minutes past eleven.

Lewis opened for the defense by explaining that he would not try to deny the fact that a terrible killing had taken place that day at Rocky Point but would provide testimony that would prove that Frank had absolutely no motive to murder his daughter.

"It takes something beyond the mere physical act of killing to produce murder," Lewis told the jury. "If Frank Sheffield were acquitted and cured today, he could never expect to enjoy life again. But to his relatives who sit in the shadows of a great grief, your verdict, gentlemen, means something.

Will you add to this sorrow the tingle of shame by branding the husband and father a felon?"

Lewis spent twenty minutes setting the stage for his arguments before Nancy was called to the witness stand and placed under oath. After she was asked to describe her husband's behavior prior to Maggie's death, she told the court that, in addition to her husband's recent unannounced trip to Attleboro, he had inexplicably wandered away from home on two previous occasions.

Nancy recounted how, the year before, he had left his home in Pawcatuck one cold, winter day and ventured out on the snow-covered ground with apparently no idea where he was going. He later explained to her that hours after he had wandered off, he came to his senses and suddenly realized that he was in Mystic, although he had no recollection of how he had gotten there.

The following month, she recalled, he disappeared from home again, this time finding himself in Preston, Connecticut. He continued on to Norwich, where he called his family and told them his whereabouts, explaining that he didn't know how he had arrived at that destination. Nancy told the court that when her husband had talked to her about his abrupt excursions, he explained that he never knew what was happening until something snapped in his head, making him rational again and able to start on his way back home.

Frank's demeanor, as the trial went on, seemed to change by the minute. The expression of despair soon turned to one that seemed to indicate little concern about what was happening around him. His apparent lack of interest in the proceedings was noticed by many who thought it odd, considering the fact that his fate was hanging in the balance. Seemingly overcome with boredom and unaware of the whispering crowd behind him, he remained strangely idle while witnesses filed passed him to take the stand and recount the events of his life for the twelve men who would determine whether he was, legally, a coldblooded killer.

George Brightman was called to the stand to give his opinion on the mental condition of his brother-in-law. George said that he believed Frank was insane and informed the court that he had even suggested to Frank's father in the past the idea of having him placed in an asylum. He testified that he had been shocked by his brother-in-law's appearance on that August day when he showed up at the house. He described Frank as looking haggard, unshaven and wearing an unnatural expression.

George stated that he was also surprised at, and concerned by, the demanding manner and urgent determination Frank exhibited as he announced repeatedly that he was taking Maggie home. "There was a peculiar glitter in his eyes when he looked at her so much that she asked him why he was staring at her that way," he testified.

Dr. George F. Keene, of the Rhode Island State Hospital for the Insane, who had finally been allowed to examine Frank in jail, told the court that he believed the defendant to be undoubtedly suffering from insanity. The forty-year-old doctor had been appointed the visiting physician of Rhode Island Institutions on March 1, 1883. He then served as deputy superintendent of the Asylum for the Chronic Insane. He would go on to be appointed superintendent of the Rhode Island State Hospital for the Insane on May 21, 1897.

Keene described in detail the psychological tests that he had performed on Frank. He then explained in a strangely confusing way how a truly insane person was likely to hurt not only his enemies but also those he loved. A person pretending to be insane, he said, usually had a violent manner and a disheveled, unkempt appearance. It wasn't immediately clear how such a testimony would help to prove that Frank was unquestionably insane, as numerous people had commented on his haggard appearance, which, according to Keene's beliefs, indicated merely a façade of insanity.

"Do you think that a man who has shown such symptoms as those that have been described and attributed to Frank Sheffield would be responsible for such acts?" Keene was asked, hypothetically.

"I would have grave doubts about such a man's responsibility," the doctor answered.

Other witnesses took the stand to give their opinions of Frank's personal appearance.

"He could hardly be recognized," stated one man who had seen him at the jail. He described Frank's face as being "all distorted and care-worn."

Hinckley spoke about the poor physical image of his friend and added that he did not expect Frank to live much longer, given his condition. Even the purser of the *Bay Queen*, who had spoken to Frank on that summer day in question, testified about his neglected face, aimless movements and vacant staring.

Still more witnesses were presented, one testifying that Frank had been fired from his job at the railroad station six months prior to the murder because of his inability to keep the freight accounts straight. In all, there were about a dozen witness testimonies for the jury to consider.

Lewis told the court that there were additional people he had planned to put under oath, but not expecting the state's case to be presented so quickly, he had not asked them to appear that day. Not wanting to prolong the

The author addresses the East Greenwich Preservation Society from the witness stand that was used at Frank Sheffield's trial. *Photograph by Marylou Fiske.*

trial, he stated that he would not ask them to appear at another time, as he believed the jury would be sufficiently convinced by the testimonies of that day of Frank's mental deficiencies.

Of all the witness statements presented that day, the most disturbing undoubtedly came from the forty-nine-year-old physician Frank had been visiting regularly at his office on High Street in Westerly. Dr. John Howard

Dr. John Howard Morgan, who knew of Frank Sheffield's
drive to kill his daughter. *Vintage photograph, author's collection.*

Morgan admitted to the court that Frank had actually been subject to past impulses to kill his daughter.

During his visits with Morgan, Frank had talked about how worried he was about not being able to hold a job. He was heavily concerned about his financial welfare and told his doctor that there were occasions when he was consumed with strife about this. At those times, he considered killing Maggie to prevent her from suffering or becoming a financial burden on someone else.

According to Morgan, Frank had a morbid fear of not being able to maintain secure employment and provide for his children. Frank had told him that, during such times of worry, he often had to struggle to keep the impulse to kill his daughter subdued. Morgan obviously had legitimate reasons to instruct Nancy not to let Frank out of her sight. However, he had failed to take any serious precautions that would prevent his patient from acting on his murderous impulses.

Morgan testified that a few days before the unspeakable crime was committed, Frank had tried to commit suicide with laudanum, a ruby-colored liquid composed of wine, saffron, cinnamon and opium. The drug was regularly prescribed for pain, and while it is possible that one of Frank's physicians prescribed it for him, there was never any mention of how he obtained it.

A man who had worked with Frank at the depot said that there were several times when Frank had told him that he was afraid his eventual death would be a fearful one. He was always despondent, said the man, and very scared of the future.

A teacher and former co-worker of Frank's at the Palmer Street School testified that although there had been times when Frank was ill and unable to carry out his duties, there was nothing about him that would have called attention to the matter any more than it would have if any other person had been feeling ill. All of the teachers and students greatly admired him, she said, and the only oddity she ever noticed was that sometimes he acted as if he was extremely nervous.

Frank's attorney put much effort into his argument that, despite his client's having taken his five-year-old child to an amusement park and killing her there, he should not be held accountable for it. There were a number of things beyond Frank's control that Lewis felt could have caused his behavior and actions on that day. He brought the court's attention to the fact that Frank had contracted a skin disease called erysipelas in 1891. Erysipelas is an infection caused by bacteria that originates in the back of a host's nose and throat. Eventually, the disease spreads to the lymphatic vessels, causing lymph node swelling, chills, fever, a distorted facial expression and a lumpy skin surface.

Preexisting factors that may lead to erysipelas are those that cause ulcerations in the back of the nose and throat, leaving a breeding ground for the bacteria. While it is not known how Frank Sheffield used cocaine—if he used it at all—snorting the drug can cause severe ulceration in that very area. Opium use, on the other hand, is known to cause dry, scaly skin and other dermatological disorders that might bring about skin ulcerations, abscesses and infections such as erysipelas.

His painful bout with the disease had left Frank in a distorted state of mind, his lawyer explained, rendering him depressed and despondent from that time on.

The defense was determined to convince the jury that Frank was not the type of man who, in a normal state of mind, would have killed his own child. He was the son of a preacher and had been known as a man of excellent character. He had a reputation for being especially kind toward children and had even held the position of school principal. He had been an innocent victim of fate and suffered a traumatic head injury from being struck by a school bell. His mind had been forever altered by a serious bacterial infection. He experienced regular involuntary lapses of memory. And besides all those things, Frank had absolutely no motive for killing his daughter. Apparently, the defense chose to completely ignore the testimony of Frank's own doctor.

There was a very important decision to be made, not only by the jurors, but also in the heads of those who knew Frank and those who had been following the case. Everyone needed to come up with their own determination concerning whether Frank was a coldblooded killer. That which the jury decided would mean his incarceration or freedom. That which the general public decided would determine his future reputation. Was Frank Sheffield truly insane? Had his mind been altered through no fault of his own by a skin problem or a blow to the head? Or was he a drug user whose habit had spiraled out of control?

"I think he is daft," was the opinion of Rocky Point Park manager Harrington.

"I don't think the man is crazy," Officer Kettle said. "I can't get it into my head that he is. It seems to me there was too much deliberation. But for his own benefit, I hope he is."

Before sending the jury out to make its decision, Judge Douglas defined for the members the crime of murder. He likened the murder of a human being committed by an insane person to that of a murder committed by a child. "There can be no criminal intent in either case," he said. "It is up to you, the jury, to decide if Frank Sheffield had criminal intent when he killed his daughter."

There was much to weigh and consider as the jury filed out of the courtroom at 2:55 p.m. However, just eight minutes later, the members returned with their verdict: not guilty, by reason of insanity.

After the jury members were excused from their duties, spectators began to leave the courtroom, some relieved and some shocked. As the room began to clear, Nancy arose and went to sit beside her husband. When she spoke to him, he smiled.

9

THE AFTERMATH

Guilt Is the Motive, Not the Result

In order for Frank Sheffield to be found not guilty of the crime of murder, he had to have legally been found to suffer from insanity. Guilty people are not let back out onto the streets, but neither are insane people. Therefore, the verdict did not free Frank back into society but earned him a bed at the Rhode Island State Hospital for the Insane, located on Howard Avenue in Cranston.

The hospital was part of the Rhode Island State Institutions complex, situated in the village of Howard. The complex was an effort to separate the poor, the insane, the feeble, the criminals and the inebriates who had all been lumped together in institutions for generations.

In 1869, the state had purchased two adjacent pieces of property: the Stukeley Westcott farm and the William Howard farm. A workhouse, an almshouse, a prison, a county jail, a reform school for boys, a reform school for girls and the hospital for the insane were built on the land. Some of the structures were of the rustic wooden variety, while others reached high into the sky, in Gothic brick-and-stone fashion. The complex, in its entirety, was managed by the Board of State Charities and Corrections.

Exactly one week after Maggie had been bludgeoned by her father behind the beautiful cliffs of Rocky Point, the matter had seemingly been all but forgotten by the vast majority of the public. On that particular day, the park had its biggest turnout of the year. A new holiday, Labor Day, had been added to the calendar, and the masses were ready to celebrate.

On that cool, crisp September morning, nearly ten thousand Rhode Islanders gathered together at half past nine to march through the streets

The Rhode Island State Hospital for the Insane, where Frank Sheffield was locked away for life. *Vintage postcard, author's collection.*

in honor of this new yearly occasion that celebrated the workingman. It had taken a great deal of petitioning to accomplish, but at last, laborers had managed to legally establish the first Monday in September as *their* day. The rhythm of drumbeats and the piercing melody of fifes set the pace for decorative floats and elated marchers to weave their way toward Dyer Street in Providence. There, on the wharves, they happily assembled to board the steamboat for Rocky Point.

The crowd that day was much larger than what had been expected, and the Continental Steamboat Company actually had to enlist the help of its competitors in order to carry the thousands of passengers down the bay to the park. Once the steamships docked, the excited masses headed toward the grove beside the park pavilion where they began a two-hour rally. A delicious clam dinner followed at the Shore Dinner Hall, and then the revelers dispersed in all directions, taking in the rides, animal menageries and performances.

The gaiety and laughter went on as usual. Nothing but a single rocky ledge separated the celebration of that day from the site of the mournful tragedy that had occurred there the week before.

On March 14, 1901, Frank died at the state hospital.

Nancy remained living in the 27 Liberty Street house for the rest of her life. By that time, she had invited her fifty-seven-year-old widowed sister, Wealthy

The grave of Frank Sheffield at Elm Grove Cemetery in Mystic, Connecticut. *Photograph by Kelly Sullivan Pezza.*

Pendleton Sisson, to come live with her. Wealthy had been married to John Edward Sisson, a veteran of the Civil War who had served in Company M of the Sixth Connecticut Artillery.

Their sixty-one-year-old brother, Charles, who had served in Company C of the First Cavalry during the Civil War, also moved in. In addition to her two children and two siblings, Nancy housed two boarders, John Wilcox and Roland B. Gavitt, who worked as machinists at a local company, and a seven-year-old girl named Lillian M. Gardner.

Nancy continued to work as a dressmaker for most of her life, visiting the homes of clients who sought her skills as a seamstress. However, in 1917, her son, Amos, who was employed as a teamster on the farm of F.L. Merritt in Noank, asked to be exempted from the draft for World War I due to the fact that he had an elderly widowed mother who was dependent on him for support.

By 1920, Amos had gained work at a local lumberyard, and the only occupants of the house at that time were himself, Nancy and Wealthy. Wealthy passed away on April 29, 1925. Nancy followed on June 25 of the following year at the age of seventy-four. Two months later, the Liberty Street house passed into the hands of a new owner.

Nancy and her sister were both laid to rest at the Thompson Family Cemetery in North Stonington, Nancy being separated from her husband even in death. Nancy, who was born on September 17, 1852, was one of nine children born to Amos Sheffield, who had died on December 4, 1888, and Sarah Warner, who had died on March 15, 1887, at the age of forty. In addition to her brother Charles, Nancy's other siblings included brothers James and Joseph, as well as four sisters: Sarah, who died in 1865 at the age of twenty-four; Mary, who died two months later at the age of nineteen; Phebe, who passed away at the age of seven in 1862; and two-year-old Harriet, who died in 1852.

Frank and Nancy's daughter, Sarah Elizabeth, went on to marry William Woodward Goff, a piano tuner, fourteen years her senior. The couple lived in Providence, Rhode Island, for a while before settling down in Westerly.

The Palmer Street School, which had been the stage for an injury that would become a subject of court testimony, was sold to the Lorraine Manufacturing Company in 1900, when the much larger West Broad Street School was constructed. Having opened its doors in 1875, Palmer Street School was initially a small institution of learning with just four classrooms and 150 students. Growing attendance necessitated the need for an addition to the building in 1890.

On September 21, 1911, the empty schoolhouse caught fire. The blaze began somewhere in the lower hallway and worked its way up three flights of stairs to the clock tower, where the bell was housed. That bell, which had apparently caused Frank a lifetime of misery, crashed down so loudly from the burning tower that it awoke half the town. By the time the flames had been put out, only one wall of the school still stood in its entirety. The other three walls remained partially standing. The entire third floor was gone, and the interior of the building contained nothing but charred wood fragments and ash.

Workmen from the manufacturing company later located the bell in the rubble. As the Pawcatuck Congregational Church of Westerly had been using a bell that was cracked, the company gave it the school bell. However, after it was installed in the church and rung, it was discovered that the heat from the fire had destroyed its tone. After being sent to a foundry, melted down and recast, it was replaced in the church belfry, where it remained until the highly destructive hurricane of 1938. Heavy winds caused the belfry to go crashing through the roof, bringing the bell down with it. As the costs for reconstruction were too high, the bell was stored away in the attic of the church.

When plans were made to raze the church in 1970 so that a gas station could be built on the property, the bell was discovered still in the attic. Plans were made to move it to the new Congregational church and place it atop a ledge in the yard.

The Kent County courthouse, where Frank's trial was held, still stands at 127 Main Street in East Greenwich. Built in 1805, it served as the seat of the Rhode Island state government until 1854 and is one of the five original statehouses in Rhode Island. The learning institute that would later become Brown University was originally established in this building, and the site also marks the location from which the first U.S. Navy was commissioned. Ownership of the building was transferred from the state to the Town of East Greenwich and underwent a total restoration. In 1995, it reopened as the East Greenwich Town Offices.

The East Greenwich jail building still stands as well. If the walls could talk, they would whisper of excuses and explanations and the great regard for the well-being of Frank Sheffield while the body of his daughter lay cold in her grave, miles away. Located at 110 King Street, it now houses the East Greenwich Preservation Society. On the lower floor of the building, the cell

The old East Greenwich jail as it looks today. *Photograph by Kelly Sullivan Pezza.*

where Frank was confined is still intact, along with the others that line the short hallway. The heavy steel doors and musty coldness of the area still feels shrouded in a dark past. Upstairs, the witness stand from the courthouse is used as a podium for meetings.

On Frank's death certificate, his cause of death is listed as "petit mal epilepsy & pulmonary laryngeal tuberculosis." Although there was a documented outbreak of tuberculosis in the institution at that time, it may or may not be coincidence that prolonged opium use made one more prone to contracting respiratory diseases.

While petit mal epilepsy is normally a childhood disorder that is usually outgrown by adulthood, one could argue that the blow to the head by the school bell caused brain damage that manifested as epileptic seizures. Such episodes, which can occur dozens of times per day, can include such symptoms as staring vacantly into space and short lapses in awareness as the brain's electrical activity is briefly disrupted. Such seizures, however, last for about thirty seconds, not the duration of time it would take for a person to walk aimlessly for miles and miles. In addition, they would not cause one to have conscious or subconscious murderous intent.

There seemed to be no definite answers to the many questions left in the wake of Maggie's death. What the world was left to understand of the tragedy was only what was documented in court transcripts and newspaper interviews. What is found there are not answers, but what seems to be a greater concern regarding the quality of life for Frank Sheffield than the five-year-old girl whose life was tragically over. From Maggie's own family, to Frank's co-workers, doctors, friends and complete strangers, thoughts seemed to center more on Frank's well-being than anything else. Virtually no one could wrap his mind around the idea of Frank knowingly committing a heinous murder. He had grown up as the son of a clergyman, raised by the word of God. He had even felt the call of the ministry himself as a young man. His early life had been perfectly normal and happy, void of tragedy or hardship. He had been a beloved teacher and school principal who was adored by those he worked with and those he taught. He fell in love, married and welcomed two beautiful children into the world, including a little girl to whom he lovingly attached himself.

Life for Frank was normal and happy up until that time. But then something unexpected happened. Something went horribly wrong. The woman he had pledged his life and love to, the woman who was supposed to help him raise those two children and remain his constant companion forever, was suddenly gone. The reason she was gone, one can calculate, was because of injuries suffered while giving birth to Maggie. Frank loved Maggie, but perhaps he loved her tragically. It was never his infant son he voiced his concerns about to friends, never his son he admitted to his doctor he was afraid of not being able to support. It was Maggie.

Sigmund Freud indicated in his theories on the human psyche that our feelings toward another person actually have nothing to do with that person. Those feelings, he believed, were innately inside us already, driven by our subconscious minds to assign them to something tangible. Perhaps the immense love Frank felt for his daughter had been first assigned to his wife before her life ebbed away, leaving him with nothing to attach it to. Perhaps he transferred those feelings to Maggie. She was, after all, the tiny female embodiment of all that he had lost.

How could Frank Sheffield, a man of such good character, willfully murder the child he loved so much? He'd had absolutely no history of violent or criminal behavior in the past. Interestingly, except in the case of serial killers, most people who commit murder have no prior criminal history. In addition, up to 85 percent of all murders are committed by a friend or relative of the victim. Why would a man kill a child he loved, even if the act was for subconscious reasons? Perhaps Frank reasoned, consciously or subconsciously, that his life had been torn apart by the death of his wife. If Mary hadn't died, he wouldn't have been forced into the throes of depression. He wouldn't have had to worry about who was going to care for his children. Perhaps he wanted to blame Mary for all that she had left him to handle alone. But he couldn't blame Mary. Mary was dead.

According to Freud's psychoanalytical research, a sense of unconscious guilt usually exists before a crime is committed, with that guilt being the motive, not the result, of the crime. He believed that people committed crimes, such as murder, to be able to fasten their guilt to something tangible, thereby providing them with final relief. Perhaps, based on Freud's theories, Frank needed to attach those feelings of blame to someone who was present.

10

THOSE LEFT BEHIND

Shadows Flee Away

Maggie's maternal grandparents raised her brother, Mason Sheffield. The couple was well to do, and Mason was provided with a privileged lifestyle. In 1898, he applied to Webb's Academy and Home for Shipbuilders, located at 188th Street in the Bronx, New York. The private undergraduate engineering college had been established by shipbuilder William Henry Webb in 1889. Having experienced the hardship of financing his own education, Webb wanted to offer young men interested in shipbuilding the opportunity to advance toward their chosen career without worrying about money. Those accepted at Webb's Academy would receive four years of training at no expense. Built of New York brownstone in the Romanesque style to resemble a castle, the academy had an attached hospital and home for the aged where elderly shipbuilders and their wives were given a place to live free of charge.

In 1902, Mason graduated from the academy, along with eleven other students. On September 14, 1910, he married twenty-nine-year-old Elsie Lenore Thorp, who had also enjoyed a lifestyle of affluence. A resident of Stonington, her father was the proprietor of a hardware store, and their family's staff at that time included two household servants.

Mason and his new wife removed to a home located at 165 Broadway in New York, where he worked as a draughtsman. The couple later relocated to 880 Clermont Street in Brooklyn, and Mason worked as a topographical draughtsman for Corporation Counsel Delany's Bureau of Street Department.

In the fall of 1916, Mason returned to Mystic, where he and his wife took up residence at the Octagon House, a two-story structure built in 1850, on West Mystic Avenue at Willow Point, and he began designing boats. They called their home Rose View Cottage, and in the summer of 1917, Elsie held a tea to celebrate a visit from Mason's aunt Mary Charlotte Brightman, who had brought along her grandson.

Later that year, Mason and Elsie removed to 5551 Pulaski Avenue in Philadelphia, Pennsylvania, where Mason was an assistant designer for an engraving company. Elise had given birth to two sons in New York, in 1915 and 1917, and by 1920, Mason was employed as a shipyard draftsman. At that time, the family was living in a rented house at 2970 North Congress Road in Camden, New Jersey. A few years later, they moved to the town of Burlington and settled into a home at 423 Cinnamonson Avenue while Mason worked as a structural engineer.

By 1933, Mason and his family were back in New York, at Pearl River and, two years later, living at 45 Adrian Avenue in New York City, where Mason worked for the Board of Water Supply, located at 346 Broadway. He passed away on June 28, 1952.

Mason Crary Hill, the man who had taken on the responsibility of raising his grandson and providing him with great opportunity, was born in the winter of 1817 in New London, Connecticut. After the tragic death of his wife, Mary Ann, and his subsequent marriage to Margaret Wheeler, he enjoyed great success brought about by his shipbuilding venture. His shipyard, located at Pistol Point at the foot of Willow Hill in Mystic, gained him such high regard that, during the Civil War, he was selected by Secretary of the Navy Gideon Welles to act as inspector of government sailing vessels. He filled the position for several years. Prior to the war, he had constructed clipper ships there at Pistol Point, among them being the *Seminole*, the *Flying Cloud*, the *Southern Lights*, the *Twilight* and the *Golden Horn*.

Business advertisements for "M.C. Hill" at Mystic Bridge stated that he provided shipbuilding in all its branches and was a dealer in oak and yellow pine, timberland plank, pure leads oil, turpentine, varnish, mixed paints and colors, glass, putty, brushes, Paris green, tar pitch, rosin, coal tar and bright varnish, oakum, caulking cotton, iron spikes, chains, anchors, wire rope and rigging and moth-proof felts. Mason also added that he was an agent for Averill, rubber and other paints and Leffert's Galvanizing.

Mason and Margaret resided at 295 York Street near the Mystic Bridge with their family. Their first child, Mary, died at the age of thirty-three in 1888. Son Charles died in 1881 at the age of twenty-five. James was born in

1858 and died in 1863. Their fourth child, son John Ethan Hill, was born in 1864, lived well into adulthood and graduated from Yale University in New Haven, Connecticut.

Daughter Lucy was born and died in 1867 with their next daughter, who was unnamed, dying the same day she was born in 1869. In 1871, son Herbert Crary Hill was born, and he also went on to graduate from Yale University. In his 1894 yearbook, he stated that although he had never researched his family history, he believed that his ancestry could be traced back to William the Conqueror. He also stated that he believed he was of English, Irish, French, Russian, Scotch and German blood. Another daughter belonging to the Hills, Maggie, died in 1874 when she was just a year old.

Mason and Margaret celebrated their fiftieth wedding anniversary on July 24, 1904. The following year, they both passed away and were laid to rest in the Hill family plot within Elm Grove Cemetery in Mystic. There, they joined Mason's first wife, the many sons and daughters they had lost all too soon and the granddaughter they had so adored in her five short years of life. Behind Mason's large grave marker is the small scroll-shaped stone erected for Maggie. To her immediate left is where her mother lies. And to the other side of Mary Ann lies Frank Sheffield.

The gravestones of Mary Ann, Maggie and Frank Sheffield at Elm Grove Cemetery in Mystic, Connecticut. *Photograph by Kelly Sullivan Pezza.*

The engraving on Mary Ann's stone reads, "Until the daybreak." Frank's stone is etched with the words "Shadows flee away," and undoubtedly there was some thought put into making a connection between Frank and Mary Ann as both epitaphs come from the King James version of the Holy Bible, Song of Solomon: "Until the day break and the shadows flee away, turn my beloved and be thou like a roe or a young hart upon the mountains of Bether."

John Franklin Sheffield, who had been the custodian of his tiny granddaughter when she was killed, was born on January 8, 1823, to John Sheffield and Eliza Lewis. At the time of Maggie's death, he had made his home at 29 Coit Street in Norwich and was pastoring at the Greenville Methodist Church. He had followed in the footsteps of his father, John, by becoming a minister. John Sr. had been a successful carriage-maker before answering the call to preach and becoming ordained to serve in the Methodist church.

The elder John's brother, Washington Wentworth Sheffield, was one of New London's leading dentists who blazed new trails in the subject of oral care. He established the International Tooth Crown Company and constructed a laboratory behind his house where he conducted experiments and invented such successful products as Dr. Sheffield's Crème Dentifrice, Dr. Sheffield's Tooth Powder and Dr. Sheffield's Elixir Balm. He is credited with being the first person to market toothpaste in a tube. By 1900, John had removed to Putnam and died there on March 8 of that year. His second wife, Mary, passed away eight years later, on January 13, 1908.

Maggie's aunt Mary Charlotte Sheffield was born on June 10, 1848, and married George Brightman on June 8, 1881, in Marshfield, Massachusetts. On September 20, 1884, she gave birth to her one and only child, Edgar Sheffield Brightman, in Holbrook. She died on May 2, 1930, shortly before her eighty-second birthday.

Edgar attended Brown University in Providence, Rhode Island, to prepare for the gospel ministry. Upon completion of his education there, he studied at the Boston University School of Theology, followed by the University of Berlin and the University of Marburg, both located in Germany. He received his PhD in Boston in 1912 and went on to teach philosophy, psychology, ethics and religion at several institutions, including Brown University, and lectured at several others, including Harvard University. Edgar had a great interest in Hinduism and was a staunch opponent of literalism in religion and irrationalism in theology.

Edgar married Charlotte Huelson on July 1, 1912, in Brooklyn, New York. She died in University Place, Nebraska, on May 24, 1915, at the age of twenty-nine, and her remains were transported to Connecticut on August 2 so that she could be laid to rest in Elm Grove Cemetery. Edgar next married Irma Baker Fall on June 8, 1918, in Middletown, Connecticut. He went on to become the father of three children and died in Newton Center, Massachusetts, in 1953.

George Brightman was born in Mystic on August 24, 1852. He united with the Methodist Episcopal Church in Mystic at the age of seventeen. He was soon licensed to begin leading meetings, and wanting to be successful in answering his call to the ministry, he entered the East Greenwich Academy so that he might prepare for college. However, for reasons unknown, he was unable to continue his education there, so he left East Greenwich in 1881 and joined the New England Southern Conference. Out of the class of ten students, he was one of only five who went on to follow a path in religion.

George's first pastorate was later in 1881, at South Braintree, Massachusetts, where he remained for three years. He went on to preach at numerous places of worship in Massachusetts, including churches in Holbrook, West Abington, Nantucket, North Dighton, Plymouth, Attleboro, Provincetown and Edgartown. His work also took him into Rhode Island, where he served churches in Providence, Newport and Pascoag. He preached in Middletown, Connecticut, as well.

While living in Edgartown, George became ill, and though he attempted to continue on with his life and career, he did not seem to be recovering from his malady. Finally, his doctor ordered him to seek a change of climate and engage in a period of rest. He did so but returned home after a while, feeling worse than he had before. While preaching his last sermon shortly before he died, everyone in attendance could see how seriously unwell George was. As his physical condition declined further, he was unable to quell the pain and often had to retire to a chair or kneel on the floor with his head rested. During this time, he would regularly speak about how much he loved his brethren in the ministry. He died in Connecticut on March 18, 1906.

Frank's brother, Charles Sheffield, was born in 1855 and married Adele Fiero when he was thirty-three years old. By 1910, the couple had removed to Huron Street in Hennepin, Minnesota, where he worked as a timekeeper in a flour mill. Charles fathered three children, and following family tradition, his eldest daughter became a teacher.

11

THE PLAYERS

Ministers, Medicine Men and Millionaires

S anford Kinnecom, the officer who transported Frank to the county jail after Maggie's death, was a lifetime resident of North Providence. In 1886, he was appointed chief of police for the North Providence Police Department, a position his father, John, had held until 1875. Eight years after the horrible killing at Rocky Point, he was employed as deputy sheriff of the Superior Court of Rhode Island. Kinnecom lived a long, active life despite the pressures of his career, and when he renewed his driver's license in 1956 at the age of ninety-two, he became one of the oldest drivers in the United States. He passed away three years later.

Reverend Smith Goodenow, one of the clergymen who presided over little Maggie's funeral service, was born in Damariscotta, Maine, on May 15, 1817. His father died when he was a child, and at the age of ten, he was sent to live with relatives in Providence, Rhode Island. He attended Waterville College (now Colby College) for three years and graduated from Bowdoin College in 1838. Five years later, he received his license to preach. In 1864, Goodenow was employed as acting principal of the English Department at Iowa. He went on to become principal of Brunswick High in Maine, a private college preparatory school. While serving as superintendent of schools in Bath, Maine, he began studying for the ministry. Goodenow preached in Connecticut, Massachusetts, Rhode Island, New York, Illinois and Iowa before dying of old age on March 26, 1897. He was buried in Battle Creek New Hope Cemetery in Ida County, Iowa.

Pardon Tillinghast, the judge who had thwarted the initial attempts of Frank's attorney to have a psychological examination of the accused conducted, was born in West Greenwich on December 10, 1836. A slender, bearded man, he was just twenty-one years old when he took over the position of principal at a local grammar school. When the Civil War broke out, he left the security of his job to enlist in the Twelfth Rhode Island Volunteers. Before long, he was made acting quartermaster. After returning from military duty, Tillinghast began his study of the law. In the early 1880s, he was associate justice for the Supreme Court of Rhode Island. Later that decade, he served as judge of the Court of Common Pleas. The year before his death, he was made chief justice of the Rhode Island Supreme Court. He died on February 9, 1905, in Pawtucket and was buried in Riverside Cemetery in that city.

Newell Belcher, one of the men whom Frank implored to turn him over to the police after killing his daughter, lived at 81 Greenwich Street in Providence at the time of the murder. He spent the greater part of his life employed at the family hardware business, Belcher & Loomis, located at 89 Weybosset Street in Providence. A Civil War veteran, he passed away on September 30, 1898, just five years after helping to turn in Frank to authorities. He was buried at Swan Point Cemetery in Providence.

Physician Moses Fifield, who had endured the horrific task of examining Maggie's dead body in the park's theater, was a native of Hartford County, Connecticut. Born on March 23, 1823, he juggled his medical career with a position at Centerville Bank in Warwick, where he was employed as a cashier for over thirty years. A round-faced gentleman with tiny spectacles, he passed away on April 9, 1900, and was interred at Centerville Methodist Cemetery.

Frank's attorney, Nathan Lewis was born on February 26, 1842, in Exeter, Rhode Island, to one of the biggest landowners of the time. His wife, Rowena Lillibridge, passed away just two months after giving birth to the last of their four children, Nathan Richmond Lewis, who was born in 1879. The baby followed his mother to the grave two years later. Lewis's first child was born in 1870 and was the only one of his children to live to adulthood. The second child was born in 1873 and died in 1874. The third was born in 1876 and died in 1877. Following his wife's death, Lewis filled the position of town clerk of Exeter and went on to become an attorney. By 1920, he had become a Second District Court judge for the State of Rhode Island. Standing at just five feet, eight inches tall, with blue eyes and dark hair, Lewis was not an intimidating man until someone was face to face with him in the courtroom. Financially successful in his chosen path, just as his father had been in his own, he took on the support of his seventy-two-year-old father-in-law, who suffered from depression after Rowena's death. The year after becoming widowed, Lewis married again, to a woman named Nettie Chester. He died in West Kingston on April 10, 1925.

Willard Tanner, the state prosecutor who had wanted nothing more than to see Frank locked away for life for murdering his daughter, maintained an office in room No. 10 at 4 Weybosset Street in Providence. A partner in the law firm Tanner & Gannon, he later went on to serve as attorney general. The Brown University graduate had a somewhat imposing presence, measuring five feet, ten inches in height, with brown eyes and brown hair. His passport application in 1899 described his facial features as "roman nose, high forehead, long face and round chin." From 1903 until 1907, he served on the auditing committee of Brown University. He went on to become a Rhode Island Superior Court judge. On May 21, 1946, Tanner passed away and was buried in Swan Point Cemetery in Providence.

Amasa Sprague, county sheriff in Warwick and one of the wealthiest men in Rhode Island, was born on December 19, 1928. His father, Amasa, owned the A&W Sprague Manufacturing Company, and the family resided in the Sprague Mansion in Cranston. In 1843, Sprague's father, Amasa Sr., was murdered on his own farm, an event that brought forth a trial that gained worldwide coverage. An Irish Catholic man named John Gordon was arrested, convicted and hanged for the crime at the state jail in Providence. It was the last hanging in Rhode Island before the death penalty was abolished. Many years later, another man confessed to the crime. Sprague's brother, Governor William Sprague, was famous for his involvement in the Civil War and for the exploits reported during his chaotic marriage and divorce. Together, the two men carried on the manufacturing company started by their father, but Amasa Jr. was sued in 1880 by his deceased niece's husband and children when they alleged that he did not distribute the holdings of Amasa Sr.'s estate as he should have. Greatly interested in horses and racing, Sprague owned the Narragansett Trotting Park. In 1874, he married a woman twenty-seven years his junior, and he died on August 4, 1902. His grave lies at Swan Point Cemetery in Providence.

Michael Lynch, who had served Frank with the warrant charging him with the murder of his daughter, was born in County Cavan, Ireland, on January 3, 1842. He came to America around the year 1862 and spent the greater portion of his life as a law enforcement officer. From 1879 to 1884, he was employed as a constable at Rocky Point Park. During the 1880s, he was also appointed special liquor constable by the Warwick Town Council. His job was to make sure all laws regarding alcohol were upheld. As the Rhode Island population was divided up between prohibitionists and anti-prohibitionists, and Lynch had friends on both sides, it was an uncomfortable position to fill. In 1899, the town council accused Lynch of failing to perform his assigned duties of closing unlicensed saloons and enforcing the closing of saloons on Sundays and neglecting to persecute persons who were selling alcohol illegally. When his attorney failed to provide evidence that he had carried out his job appropriately, the town council removed him from his position. The loss of his job was humiliating for the distinguished-looking officer who maintained a scowling look of seriousness on his face at all times. When he was reappointed to the position in 1901, he took great measures to live up to the standards that had been set for him. From 1902 to 1929, he served as deputy sheriff of Kent County, taking the place of the deceased Amasa Sprague. On November 14, 1920, just after five o'clock in the evening, Lynch was seriously injured after leaving the Kent County Superior Courthouse and following a fellow attorney across the street to a waiting automobile. Just as he approached the car, a motorcyclist with a passenger in its sidecar struck Lynch and knocked him to the ground. A resident of Tollgate Road in Apponaug, Lynch retired as chief of police in 1929 and passed away on February 3, 1933. Two of his sons, as well as his grandson, went on to work as constables at Rocky Point.

John Morgan, the Westerly physician who knew of Frank's overpowering urge to murder his own daughter and who may or may not have relayed that bit of information to his patient's wife or family, was born in Pendleton, Connecticut, on January 30, 1844. He worked as a clerk at the Westerly Post Office before enlisting for the Civil War in Company B of the Ninth Rhode Island Volunteers on May 26, 1862. After several months serving as company clerk, he reenlisted and was assigned to Company H of the Twenty-sixth Connecticut Volunteers. He was later appointed second sergeant of that company. Upon his release from the army on August 17, 1863, he went back home to Connecticut, where he gained employment as a cashier at National Niantic Bank. The following year, he entered the University of New York to engage in the study of medicine. After his graduation in 1868, he interned as an assistant physician for a year at Blackwell's Island Hospital for Incurables. Located on one end of Roosevelt Island in Manhattan, the Gothic-looking charitable institution provided medical care to the poor, as well as to the inmates confined in the prison on the other side of the island. During the later part of 1869 and early 1870, Morgan interned as a house physician at the New York Hospital for Epileptics & Paralytics. He maintained a private practice in New York City from 1870 until 1879 and then moved to Rhode Island and opened a practice in Westerly, where he specialized in psychological medicine and nervous diseases. In 1884, he was appointed the first medical examiner for that town. The physician wrote several papers that appeared in medical journals concentrating on subjects such as diphtheria, aneurisms and spinal cord injuries. He co-founded the Washington County Medical Society and, in time, served as its president, secretary and treasurer. He also served as president of the Westerly Physicians Association. Morgan resided at 43 High Street in Westerly. He had spent two weeks visiting his daughter, Mrs. Charles F. Richards, at her home on Wheeler Street in Orange, New Jersey, when he suffered a cerebral hemorrhage and died there on the evening of June 20, 1913.

12

THE SITE

Fires, Lawsuits and Baseball

D eath at Rocky Point didn't end in 1893. In the summer of 1905, the body of a man was discovered in a secluded area of the park. He was later identified as forty-two-year-old Fred Bruemel of Paterson, New Jersey. A saloonkeeper who had been married for fifteen years and the father of a fifteen-year-old son, he had committed suicide by shooting himself in the head. This would also not be the last death at the park.

Running a large attraction like Rocky Point was a major task, but Harrington did so successfully while also taking over the management of its competition, Crescent Park, in 1907. Crescent Park was another massive amusement resort situated along Narragansett Bay in the town of Riverside. Harrison called it the "Coney Island of the East" and, just as he did at Rocky Point, served shore dinners that packed visitors into the dinner hall. Harrington kept the midway at Crescent Park interesting with an underground river, electrical illusions, moving pictures, a Parisian carnival and a human roulette wheel.

In 1910, Harrington was denied a license to serve liquor at Crescent Park on Sundays and obtained a lawyer to argue about the repercussions of such a decision. He had welcomed over 700,000 people to the park the previous year and feared that if the workingman was unable to procure a drink when he wanted to, his crowds would dwindle in number. Despite his lawyer's protests, Crescent Park was forced to remain dry on Sundays.

That same year, on November 10, Harrington bought Rocky Point Park outright from the Providence, Fall River & Newport Steamboat Company,

Crescent Park, Rocky Point's competition. *Vintage postcard, author's collection.*

which had purchased it from the American Steamboat Company, for $250,000. He had initially offered to buy the property for $150,000, but the steamboat company rejected the offer, necessitating Harrington to raise the amount he was willing to pay.

Rides and attractions never before available for the enjoyment of New Englanders were brought in, and it seemed to everyone that Rocky Point would never stop outdoing itself or its competitors. Ferris wheels, roller coasters, a swimming area and a small railroad were attractions now drawing the masses to the seaside resort. The Gypsy's Cave, the Mystic Moorish Maze, flying sleighs, underground river, electrical parlors, Oriental Past-times, giant Parisian Carousel and the Japanese Garden were just the tip of the iceberg when it came to all there was to do and see. There was also vaudeville, theater productions, band performances and dancing for the enjoyment of the crowds who visited.

By 1911, Rocky Point Park had far less competition than it had in the past. Crescent Park was now the only other large public shore resort along the Narragansett Bay. Field's Point had been driven out of business due to a government decision to enlarge shipping accommodations along the upper part of the waterway. It eventually became the site for a municipal pier and a sewage treatment plant. Vanity Fair and Boyden Heights closed

The Ferris wheel at Rocky Point was a favorite destination for those seeking a breathtaking view and thrills at the same time. *Vintage postcard, courtesy Jules Antiques & General Store.*

Field's Point, where Charles Lyon perfected the art of the clambake. *Vintage postcard, author's collection.*

down when the high cost of clams raised the price of their seafood dinners and reduced business.

Success didn't come to Harrington without its obstacles, however. The deeply religious residents of Rhode Island not only had tried to stop the Sunday baseball games at the park but also felt that dancing on the Sabbath needed to be cut out. On Memorial Day weekend, police commissioner Patrick Quinn decided to go take a walk around Rocky Point. There, he spotted a police officer who had been detailed for duty at the park standing near the entrance of the pavilion dance hall. After engaging in conversation with the officer, Quinn learned that a dance was scheduled to be held at noontime. Quinn informed the officer, as well as park authorities, that no dancing would be allowed. Whether the event took place that day as planned, regardless of Quinn's forbidding it, is not known. However, dancing at Rocky Point continued for decades.

A new addition to the amusements that year was the Scenic Mountain Railway ride, built by Lamarcus Thompson, a slow-moving roller coaster that carried passengers through and over dark tunnels that replicated the Rocky Mountains. Measuring 150 feet longer than any other railway or roller coaster, it was the longest ride in all of New England.

The Palm Garden, the Rivers of Venice, the Rattlesnake Den and an $8,000 organ that reproduced the effect of a sixty-piece band were a few

Rocky Point's scenic railway. *Vintage postcard, courtesy Jules Antiques & General Store.*

more of the attractions amid the hundreds of rides, amusements and exhibits scattered over the grounds.

L.B. Walkers "Diving Girls" provided park patrons with something to marvel at as they performed their amazing swimming and diving feats. Helen Kuntzler, a sixteen-year-old member of the group, swam from Patience Island to Rocky Point, a distance of four and half miles in one hour and fifty-three minutes. The following week, she swam to Rocky Point from Crescent Park.

The dance hall filled up quickly on cool summer evenings when James J. Lamb and his musicians swelled the ballroom with melody. Only in his thirties, Lamb had begun taking violin lessons at the age of fifteen and organized Lamb's Band & Orchestra at the age of twenty-two. He would provide popular entertainment for the patrons of Rocky Point Park on a regular basis for over ten years.

The ball field remained a favorite destination of park visitors, and on July 16 of that year, shock befell a crowd of hundreds when a man was accidentally killed there. Private chauffer William Fort of Boston had driven his employer, William Hunter, and three of his friends to the park earlier that day to watch the ballgame. He had parked his automobile alongside several others in the tall grass not far from the entrance to the ball field. As the end of the game neared, Fort went to the car, started it up and backed out of the parking space. It was not until a witness informed him that he realized he had just run over a man. Fifty-eight-year-old Providence carpenter Hiram P. Bangs had lain down to take a nap in the tall grass near the field some time earlier, and his chest had been crushed by a rear wheel of Fort's auto. Someone immediately told the officials at the ballpark what had just transpired, and the ballgame was stopped. A doctor was summoned and arrived quickly, but Bangs expired just three minutes later.

Another accident resulting in death occurred at the park the following summer. A man named Thomas Martin and three of his friends, all from Taunton, Massachusetts, had come to Rocky Point that June day, intending to watch the ballgame scheduled to take place. The car Martin was driving was new, and he had yet to get used to its mechanisms. He turned into the parking area near the dance hall and attempted to back the car into a parking spot along the iron fence that served as a sea wall. However, when he reached down to pull the brake handle, he accidentally pulled the reverse handle instead, and the car catapulted through the twenty-foot-tall fence and spun up into a compete somersault before landing at the bottom of a rocky cliff.

All four men were thrown from the vehicle onto the rocks. Martin and two of his friends escaped with injuries: William Hartigan sustained a fractured elbow, Joseph Mahoney suffered a fractured left knee and Martin walked away with bruises. But another friend, Thomas Brady, who lived at 113 Winthrop Street, was pinned beneath the car. Harrington saw the accident and rushed with several other men to the scene. They were able to lift the car and extricate Brady, who was employed as a clerk at a meat market in Taunton, Massachusetts, but they could see that he was badly hurt. An ambulance was summoned, and Brady was transported to Rhode Island Hospital, where it was discovered that he had a fractured pelvis. He died four hours later.

In 1912, Casey's Fun Factory was added to the park grounds, offering twenty shows for the price of one admission, and entertainment at the Forest Casino, managed by John H. Thornton, included Jolly John Harrison singing old Irish ballads in his rough brogue and wood-shoe dancers Skinner & Woods. A costume contest in August brought lots of laughs, and the winner was John Roth, who was awarded a silver loving cup for donning a red, white and blue silk lady's garment.

The following year, the Shore Dinner Hall was expanded to allow comfortable seating accommodations for 2,500 people. It was open from noon to eight o'clock at night. Some of the delicious clams served there

The beach at Rocky Point drew not only day visitors but also those who bought cottages so they could spend several weeks at the shore. *Vintage photograph, author's collection.*

were brought in from sandy beaches in Maine, and others were supplied by John Henry Northup, an Apponaug fisherman who was in his sixties. Two different sized meals were available: the fifty-cent shore dinner and the larger seventy-five-cent dinner, prepared by Charles E. Lyon. Born on February 28, 1845, in Woodstock, Connecticut, the talented caterer had worked as a horse clipper until 1900. He went on to become a co-founder of the S.S. Atwell Catering Company, along with Gilbert Luter and Colonel Seagur Schuyler Atwell. Atwell was a well-known Civil War army commander and had long worked as a caterer, cooking up shore dinners on a regular basis at Field's Point, a thirty-seven-acre park in Providence, which he began leasing in 1887.

The Atwell company was incorporated in 1907 "for the purpose of engaging in the business of conducting and furnishing shore dinners, catering to and owning, leasing, operating and managing hotels and restaurants, and of carrying on any business connected with or incident to any of the forgoing purposes." In addition to regularly catering meals at Field's Point, the trio and its staff did occasional catering at institutions such as the Oaklawn School for Girls. In 1911, Lyon took over the company and moved the entire staff to Rocky Point Park. He later passed away in New London, Connecticut, in 1932.

Rocky Point's scenic railway and massive organ. *Vintage postcard, courtesy Jules Antiques &*
General Store.

Rocky Point's café and bandstand. *Vintage postcard, courtesy Jules Antiques & General Store.*

A large advertisement ran in the local newspapers that summer for "Col. A. Harrington's Rocky Point." In addition to listing the many rides and attractions, Harrington went on to state, "I run Rocky Point so as to make a pleasure park where women and children can come without any escort, where they can enjoy plenty of harmless amusements without danger of molestation."

Running a successful amusement park like Rocky Point wasn't all fun and games. On April 26, 1913, Harrington hired the beautiful twenty-nine-year-old pioneer female aviator and airplane exhibitionist Ruth Bancroft Law to perform a show on the park grounds for three consecutive days. According to the contract, Ruth would exhibit her spiral flying stunts on May 30 and 31 and June 1 at the park's ball field, making two flights per day and flying a total of thirty minutes per day, for a total of $1,200. Harrington was to pay Law $300 when she arrived at the park on May 30 with her specially constructed biplane and an additional $300 on completion of her performances each day.

When Law arrived, Harrington handed over the first $300 payment. Law later rose up into the air to begin performing her aerobatics, but after just three minutes into her exhibition, a heavy gust of wind hurled the plane out of the sky and into a nearby automobile, damaging the flying machine. Obviously the show was over. However, when Harrington asked for the return of his money, Law refused, and a legal battle ensued.

The scenic railway at Rocky Point Park. *Vintage postcard, courtesy Jules Antiques & General Store.*

Entertainment in the sky was very popular with patrons of Rocky Point, and several aviators appeared in shows there above the sprawling park grounds. On June 30, 1913, Swedish-born Nels J. Nelson, a twenty-six-year-old "birdman" who resided in New Britain, Connecticut, arrived at the park with his new seventy-horsepower hydro airplane. Never having been exhibited before in Rhode Island, it entertained crowds throughout the Fourth of July weekend.

Starting out on the beach in front of the Mansion House, Nelson's plane raced across the water until it picked up enough speed to glide up into the sky. Three flights were planned, with Nelson leaving the grounds of Rocky Point at ten minutes past ten o'clock in the morning, circling the city hall, the fire station and the statehouse and returning back to the park at thirty minutes past ten. The crowds below went wild.

Another famous aviator, Frank John Terrell, also gave a performance at the park that summer. The forty-five-year-old would be killed the following year when his Curtiss Pusher plane collapsed at five hundred feet in the air and plunged to the ground as he swerved to avoid hitting the audience gathered at the fairgrounds in Chesterfield, South Carolina. Terrell was buried in the wreckage and died immediately. Later that day, upon learning of the accident, his daughter sent a Western Union telegram to her aunt that read, "Papa killed today. Machine collapsed."

Rex Natator, the only man who had ever successfully swum the Niagara Rapids and who had made numerous attempts to swim the English Channel, was scheduled to swim from the Seekonk River boathouse to Rocky Point. As Natator had just recovered from pneumonia, it was expected to be a trying feat. Standing at just five feet, six inches tall and weighing just 130 pounds, Natator was able to expand his chest by eleven inches when he inhaled.

That year, the park's ball field became the site of the first automobile polo game ever played in New England and drew a crowd of over 2,500 people. The game featured four cars being stationed in the center of the field, with each carrying a driver and a polo player leaning out of the auto with a mallet. A ball was placed on the ground between the cars, and two Americans challenged two Canadians for the win.

That same summer saw the addition of a new ride called the Scranton Coal Mine, which carried passengers through dark tunnels and down a deep shaft to view the work of coal miners in action. Twenty-seven Mexican burros had been imported from Mexico to pull the two-seated cars through the mine. The expense for this was great, and the trip from Mexico to

Rhode Island took three months. Unfortunatly, five of the burros making the journey died before reaching their destination.

The animals arrived in Providence in June with their owner, W.A. "Snake" King, a resident of Tampa, Mexico, who maintained about two thousand burros on his ranch, El Víbora. King's journey through Mexico, Texas and on to Providence, Rhode Island, was life threatening. As he passed through the battlefields of a Mexican rebellion, he was forced to venture thirty-five miles off course to keep out of the line of fire. However, while on this route, as he attempted to pass through one town, he found its perimeters had been secured with live electrical wires to keep anyone from entering or exiting. The dead bodies of Mexican soldiers lay sprawled across the fields and the burros in his custody carefully paraded through them. During a stop to pick up supplies, King later related that he saw unspeakable scenes. As the government had taken control of the area, available food had become nearly nonexistent. Residents had been surviving on snakes for about two weeks.

Upon delivering the animals to Rocky Point, King told Harrington that if he wanted any more burros in the future, he would have to go get them himself. At the park, the burros were trained to carry passengers through the mine by the act of tying bundles of hay to a stick suspended just in front of their mouths. In an effort to reach the hay, the burros would keep walking forward.

Adding to the year's summer fun, champion runner Bart Sullivan engaged in a relay race on the grounds, and Torrelli's Dog and Pony Circus gave four open-air performances, starring six ponies, five dogs and the badly behaved Bessie, the mule. Any patron who wanted to try his or her luck at staying on Bessie's back while she bucked around was invited to come up and give it his or her best shot. It was promised that anyone who could do so would win the mule as a prize.

The Forest Casino had advertised an exciting bill for the season. Beulah Ballas was scheduled to perform her well-known southern songs and African American melodies, and comedian Frank Dobson would take the stage. Blackface comics Kelly & Davis had shows coming up, as did character comedian Nellie Fillimore and soprano Isabella Hackley.

One of the Forest Casino's most popular performances that year was given by Mademoiselle Emerie, a Parisian trapeze artist who was well known for her shockingly provocative shows. Emerie would begin her performances on the stage, dressed in full evening garb. A male assistant would then bring her a glass of wine, which she would drink before pretending to become intoxicatingly carefree. She would climb the ladder that led to the trapeze and begin disrobing while she sailed through the air. Her shows were said to be sidesplitting entertainment, and she always ended each performance clad only in tights. Other performances were given by the Bush Devere Trio, which starred cornet and violin player Billy Bush, and Clinton & Beatrice, who put on an exhibition of fancy rifle shooting.

High-wire acts on the grounds always garnered large audiences. These included the Savolas, a pair of trick-riding bicyclists known as "the two demons" who always dressed in their customary devilish costumes.

On Labor Day weekend 1913, several contests were held for the enjoyment of visitors, with prizes awarded at different attractions in the park. The Scenic Railway was giving away a Mexican burro and saddle. The Scranton Coal Mine was awarding two tons of coal to a lucky winner. A barrel of flour could be won at the Forest Casino, a barrel of onions and a barrel of potatoes at the Democrat Inn and a gold watch and graphaphone at the dance hall.

Despite how well business was going, Harrington soon found himself in court once again. That October, he appeared with his attorney at the Rhode Island Superior Court to give testimony concerning an event that had occurred in the summer of 1909. One of the park's patrons, William A. Rice, claimed that he had been assaulted and wrongly confined on the park grounds by a park constable who was also an off-duty Warwick police officer. He was asking to be awarded $10,000 in damages. Harrington argued that Rice had been creating a great deal of noise and causing a disturbance, so it had become necessary to arrest him and take him to the park's confinement cell, which Sprague had previously constructed on the property for holding inebriated patrons. Despite Harrington's arguments regarding Rice's alleged inappropriate behavior, the court ruled in favor of the plaintiff.

The ravages of yet another fire occurred on May 4, 1914, when, just after five o'clock in the morning, a man working on the grounds saw smoke billowing out of the window of the penny vaudeville building. A bucket brigade was quickly formed, and the Conimicut Fire Company was summoned, but the blaze continued on for several hours, destroying the vaudeville building, the peanut stand, shooting gallery, fishpond and two unoccupied stands. Most of the concessions that were ruined were owned by a Canadian man named John B. Nash, who spent over half a century in the amusement park business. As poor luck would have it, he suffered the greatest part of the $12,000 to $15,000 loss. While much of it could be rebuilt, that which could not bore its sad damage. The many beautiful shade trees that lined the midway were permanently blemished with scorch marks. However, business went on as usual.

The newly constructed Motor Drome, a large motorcycle racetrack set at a forty-degree angle, proved very popular with visitors. In June, a racing performance was given there by European champion Daredevil McFee and Seymore Blockder of Australian racing fame. During the thrilling show, an employee who wasn't aware that a race was taking place opened a trapdoor beneath the track that hit the front wheel of McFee's motorcycle. As McFee had been driving at a speed of seventy miles per hour, his cycle veered sharply, and he was thrown violently to the ground. The racer did not get up for several moments, and many feared he was badly injured. But he came away from the accident with nothing more than a few bruises.

Crowds turned out for popular shows such as the one put on by the Balton Troupe from Paris. A group of aerial performers, it consisted of five women and one man. With their trapeze erected to the right of the Mansion House, they performed amazing stunts that had the crowd gasping. One of the female performers, who was extremely heavyset, hung from the trapeze by her knees, forty feet above the ground. In her hands, she held the end of a rope that was secured on the other side. A series of trapezes was suspended from the rope, and the other aerialists performed their feats on them.

For those who liked real nail-biting entertainment, the performance by Mademoiselle Tardieu was the show to see. Seated in an automobile that had been hoisted to the top of a forty-foot-high tower, the brave young woman

The amusements at Rocky Point Park never failed to entertain and impress. *Vintage postcard, courtesy Jules Antiques & General Store.*

would swing downward, make a revolution and then swing back upward, where the car was released from its restraints to go sailing through the air. Before landing on an inclined platform fifty-five feet away from the tower, the lady and her vehicle would complete a somersault thirty feet above the ground.

While memories were being made at Rocky Point, so was history. Thirty veterans of the Civil War held their forty-second annual outing at the park that July, all former members of the Seventh Rhode Island Volunteers. Among the group was fifty-six-year-old Francis Edwin Elwell, a famed sculptor.

Elwell had sculpted the Seventh Regiment's monument at Smith Granite Company in Westerly, Rhode Island, from blue Westerly granite. The statue, which depicts an infantryman who has picked up the fallen colors, represents the state's lone regiment in the Vicksburg Campaign. It was erected at a cost of $5,000 and stands in the Vicksburg National Military Park.

Orphaned at the age of four, Elwell was reportedly adopted by author Louisa May Alcott. He received his initial instruction in art from her sister Abigail and went on to become curator of ancient and modern sculpture at the Metropolitan Museum of Art in New York City. When he later had a disagreement with a museum official, he was fired from his position there and escorted off the property by a police officer.

In 1901, the government of Rhode Island had made Elwell an honorary colonel of the Seventh Regiment. He passed away eight years after this visit to Rocky Point while waiting for a streetcar in Connecticut.

Throughout the years, aviators continued to perform at the park, taking to the skies over the bay and eliciting oohs and ahs from the crowds watching from below. In May, Jack McGee of Pawtucket put on a great show for park patrons. The twenty-nine-year-old flew his Burgess-Wright biplane to a height of 1,500 feet so that acrobat Monsieur Burnette could drop out secured to a parachute. Burnette landed on the water directly in front of the park's Mansion House.

Prior to becoming a famed flyer, McGee had worked as a boxer, elevator operator, jewelry tradesman, automobile mechanic and chauffer. He had signed up for flying lessons in Massachusetts, but the school closed before he had completed his training. Regardless, he purchased his own plane and made his first solo flight just two years before his performance at Rocky Point. In 1917, he went to work as a test pilot for Gallaudet Aircraft Corporation. Just after eight o'clock on the morning of June 13, 1918, he was testing out a seaplane on Greenwich Bay in East Greenwich when a gust of wind upset his machine as it skipped along the water. The plane nose-dived twenty-five feet to the bottom of the bay, and McGee was drowned. His body was found badly tangled in the wreckage of the plane seven hours later by a dredging company diver.

In addition to the rides, attractions and shows, contests were still very popular at Rocky Point. A dance contest, which took place in August, was won by popular vote by twenty-year-old Normal Joseph Verrier of Arctic and sixteen-year-old Mabel Grace O'Neil of Providence. The couple walked away with an exquisite silver loving cup as their prize.

Being a fantasyland of caves, coves, gardens and groves, the natural beauty of Rocky Point Park easily rivaled its man-made entertainments. Of the many promenades located on the grounds, the one that proved to be the most enjoyed by guests was the boardwalk that ran along the bluff. While strolling there, visitors could enjoy the incredible portrait nature had painted. Once filled with the wonder of the beautiful landscape, they could continue on to the end of the bluff, where they approached a shop offering refreshments, candy and cigars.

The staff on the grounds that year included James J. Lamb as manager of the dance hall; George Krokorian, who was in charge of refreshments; Charles Lyon as dinner hall manager and his son Sumner Edward Lyon as assistant dinner hall manager; John Fontaine, who ran the photography studio; L.A. Davis as foreman farmer; Ernest Smith as superintendent of the grounds; Charles Hill as manager of the Mansion House; and Anna C. McElroy as the manager of the quick lunch stand.

That year, the price of the lobster bake had risen to sixty cents, and modern-day women known as suffragists took to the grounds of Rocky Point to make speeches about women's right to vote.

Three years later, the Monkey Speedway was added to Rocky Point. Located inside a circular tent near the park entrance at the south end of the midway, it showcased six chimpanzees driving tiny automobiles at great speeds.

Also new was a ride called the Teaser, placed at the north end of the midway near the trolley loop. The ride consisted of two seats facing each other, with a steering wheel in between them. As riders spun the wheel, they were moved up and down and twirled in circles.

The Eden Musée, a collection of wax figures bearing the likenesses of famous people, was also stationed in the building opposite the dinner hall.

Among the entertainment that summer was the Six Flying Herberts, a group of aerialists who performed dangerous high dives and triple somersaults on three trapezes suspended thirty-five feet in the air, and the return of Walker's Diving Girls. The regular Sunday baseball games played at the park featured teams such as the Boston Beaneaters and the Toronto

Popular music and amusing contests often brought a full house to Rocky Point Park's dance hall. *Vintage postcard, Courtesy Jules Antiques & General Store.*

Maple Leafs. However, despite the huge draw they brought in, the games continued to be a thorn in the sides of those who felt that such things should be abstained from on the Sabbath. Finally, three Warwick residents and a local reverend took it on themselves to visit the statehouse, where they appealed to the governor to stop the Sunday baseball games being held on the park grounds. The governor assured them that he would put a stop to baseball taking place anywhere in Rhode Island on Sundays, once and for all. "If the Warwick Police Commission can't stop Sunday baseball at Rocky Point, I can," he announced. Success in that endeavor was not found.

There had already been very vocal movements geared toward aborting the games, including one in 1889 and another in May 1911, when Reverend W.S. McIntyre of the Lord's Day League of New England organized efforts to stop park owners from disrespecting the Sabbath. Most Rhode Islanders loved their baseball, however, and flocked to the ball field week after week to watch the Cherokee Indians and several other professional-league teams. On September 27, 1914, Babe Ruth had pitched for the Providence Grays when they played against the Chicago Cubs, hitting what should have been a home run out into Narragansett Bay. However, under the rules of the game, it was not regarded as such.

Unfortunately, by the beginning of autumn, the ball field had lost its pristine image as the perfect place to view Sunday sports. Harrington had become ill and was unable to keep up the grounds as he had in the past. The Providence Grays, like many other major-league teams that had been playing at the park, expressed their feelings regarding the ball field's being unsatisfactory for the future. They decided to stop holding their games there and find a new venue. The last professional baseball game at Rocky Point took place on September 9, 1917.

13

THE HAND OF FATE

Hurricanes and Other Disasters

Harrington died in 1918, leaving his family to decide the fate of Rocky Point. His widow, Amelia, leased the park to Paul and Alfred Castiglioni later that year, but like others who had taken over what appeared to be a risk-free opportunity, they would soon learn that events of misfortune occurring at the shore resort were not over. In 1919, the beautiful Mansion House caught fire and burned to the ground.

Despite the setback, it was necessary that Rocky Point continue to evolve if it was going to keep its stellar reputation. A major overhaul took place the following year when a new bathing beach was laid out and $50,000 spent to add a new pavilion.

By that time, the large variety of rides included the Witching Waves, two merry-go-rounds, a midway carousel, a roller coaster, the Whip, the Circle Swing and the Aero Plane. While admission to the park was still free, each ride and most attractions and exhibits now required the purchase of a ticket. Entrance to theater shows cost patrons ten cents. The majority of the rides called for six-cent tickets.

Other enjoyments to be found included the Alligator Farm, the World's Museum and *Leo the Lion*, the large cast-iron statue situated at the park's entrance where many a child climbed atop to have his or her picture taken. The lion was later moved to the beach near the boat landing before vandals destroyed it.

The new wooden Wildcat roller coaster was added in 1926, and in 1931, a bobsled coaster called the Flying Turns was installed on the grounds, both

A view of Rocky Point Park from Narragansett Bay. *Vintage postcard, courtesy Jules Antiques & General Store.*

Rocky Point's dock was busy all day loading and unloading thousands of passengers. *Vintage postcard, courtesy Jules Antiques & General Store.*

designed by Herbert Schmeck. The Flying Turns resembled a bobsled run with banked curves void of a track. The Tunnel of Love was also introduced for those who wanted a heart-pounding experience of another kind.

Those who wished to experience the thrill of amusements like coasters and swings gladly handed over their ten cents. Paul S. Haney filled the position of office manager at the time, though he later went on to become employed at Crescent Park.

In August 1930, the park was put in a rather unflattering light when the *Afro-American*, a newspaper published in Baltimore, Maryland, accused Rocky Point's owner and staff of practicing discrimination. "Rocky Point Amusement Company bars colored people from the bathing beach and swimming pool," the article read. It went on to explain that the Young Men's Bible Class of the Ebenezer Baptist Church had held its annual outing there at the park earlier that month. Of the fifteen-member class, two of the men had gone and requested towels and lockers at the bathhouse. It was alleged that the men were told by the attendant there that the management would not allow lockers to be rented to those of African American descent.

"For many years, it's been the custom of thousands of blacks from New England and New York to gather at Rocky Point on August 1, to celebrate the freedom of West Indian slaves by England," the article went on. "This year, over five thousand gathered but not a single one was seen in bathing." It was further alleged that the saltwater pool had been drained dry by the management to avoid having to refuse entrance to African Americans who expressed a desire to swim.

If a reputation for bigotry was not enough, fate had even more in store for Rocky Point. Though the incredible seaside location made for a perfect park setting, it also made the grounds likely to fall victim when severe weather threatened. On September 21, 1938, a massive hurricane that no one was prepared for swept across New England, wreaking havoc with a wind speed of 160 miles per hour. Over six hundred deaths were reported, along with more than $300 million in damages. The erosion of dunes and beaches and the obliteration of hundreds of buildings changed the landscape overnight. New England had never before seen such unimaginable death and destruction.

The majority of the buildings and rides contained within Rocky Point were reduced to splinters and twisted metal fragments by the crashing waves and heavy, violent winds. The Wildcat and the Flying Turns were gone. The midway was gone and the dinner hall swept away. The storm's ravaging of the property was so severe that Rocky Point was shut down in its entirety.

The previous year, six monkeys had escaped from their confines in the park and were residing in the woods just outside the grounds. Having survived the hurricane, the monkeys continued to be seen for several months, enjoying their freedom as they swung through the trees and perched on branches just beyond the reach of captivity.

Following the devastation, the Castiglionis decided to return their lease to Mrs. Harrington, who then leased the grounds to Thomas F. Wilson of Providence in 1939. It was reopened briefly in 1940 but then closed once again, without Wilson's completing the restorations.

Mrs. Harrington decided to sell the property in 1941 but had little luck with that endeavor. Interested developers were no longer so eager to purchase the grounds once they discovered the enormous amount of rock that was contained on the property and the expense it would require to blast through it all.

There were, in fact, some very interested buyers in the form of oil companies who wanted to build oil tanks on the property. However, Mrs. Harrington could not stand the thought of the beautiful landscape being destroyed.

In 1945, the property was purchased by the Studley Land Company and, two years later, transferred to Rocky Point Incorporated, a partnership between Frederick Hilton, Joseph Trillo and Providence businessman Vincent Ferla. Along with his friends and family, Ferla put the park back in motion. The efforts took massive amounts of time and money. Aside from the basic cleanup of the park, it was necessary to rebuild structures that had been destroyed. A new Shore Dinner Hall was constructed and run by head chef John Gomes and a staff of two hundred. Measuring 260 feet by 80 feet, the all-wood building was set 30 feet farther out over the sea than the previous hall had been. Solidly built and set on nearly two hundred concrete piers, it was believed the structure could withstand almost any surge of water or gust of wind. To be on the safe side, however, hurricane insurance was taken out on the building.

The saltwater swimming pool, which had sustained damage, was renovated, and a new dance hall called the Palladium was constructed. However, despite all the rebuilding and renovations, when Rocky Point was opened once again to the public, it did not garner as much success as it had in times past. The country's economic hardships had brought about a decline in people spending money on such frivolous things as rides and games of chance. In April 1953, the park advertised that it was selling the Rocket ride and the Whip together for $17,500. The shining light that had once been Rocky Point seemed as if it were starting to dim.

Though local newspapers no longer carried large, exciting advertisements for the once prosperous summer playground, they occasionally mentioned the park in other news. In August, a trio of men who were out boating in the bay had been fishing near Prudence Island when suddenly their outboard motorboat banged up against something in the water. Immediately, they spotted a twelve-foot practice missile for which the navy had been looking for the past four days. The men towed the missile to the dock at Rocky Point, and navy officials in Newport were contacted. Soon, a boat carrying ten enlisted men arrived, and the men hoisted the missile aboard to bring it back to Newport. The usual payout for the return of a missile was $100.

One year later, Ferla and his partners would find themselves the next unfortunate victims of Rocky Point's regularly unexpected tragedies. On August 31, 1954, Hurricane Carol crashed into the East Coast with ninety-mile-per-hour winds. Again, many of the park's rides were almost completely destroyed, as was the newly built Shore Dinner Hall.

The owners of the park sustained over $25,000 in losses and charged the J.L. Campbell Insurance Company with forcing them to simply endure the situation. Vincent Ferla claimed that he had instructed the insurance company to place $82,000 worth of insurance with the Guaranty Fire & Marine Insurance Company and to supplement it with insurance from other companies. Ferla charged that the company had failed to follow those instructions.

The devastation came on the heels of yet another lawsuit, this one brought against the park owners by the owner of the Gowell Amusement Company, which owned the Tumblebug ride operated at Rocky Point. He testified that he had originally purchased the ride in Pennsylvania for $13,000 and that he brought it to Rocky Point in 1928, where he operated it for many years under the agreement that he was to give the owners of the park 25 percent of the gross income he earned giving rides to patrons.

The Tumblebug, which was a machine holding six cars that rotated on a circular wooden track around a center spindle, was put up for sale in 1938 by the City of Warwick when the owner became delinquent in his company's property taxes. The owner repurchased the ride, created by the Traver Engineering Company, from the city with the intention of continuing its operation at Rocky Point, but then the park closed down.

To keep the motors safe, the ride owner placed them in storage at a local machine company but left the remainder of the ride on the park grounds. In 1947, when the park changed hands again, all property, including land and buildings became that of a new owner. Some of the rides and concessions

The bug ride at Rocky Point. *Vintage postcard, courtesy Jules Antiques & General Store.*

were privately owned, and they were listed on the agreement as being such, not part of the property transferal. The Tumblebug, however, was not listed.

The owner of the ride was notified to come remove it from the park, but he expressed his wish to return to its operation under the same agreement he had followed previously. Frederick Hilton was not agreeable to that and stated that he wanted a flat $3,000 yearly fee. When no agreement could be reached, Hilton had repairs made to the ride and sold it for $8,500. The new owner agreed to let the ride remain at the park and pay Hilton's desired $3,000 annual fee.

The previous owner claimed in court that the ride belonged to him and, before repairs, had been worth a little over $6,000. Hilton claimed its actual worth had been more like $500. The court ruled in favor of the ride's previous owner and awarded him $3,500. Hilton's appeal for a new trial was denied.

Then came the hurricane and, with it, stark reality for those now faced with the seemingly never-ending task of putting Rocky Point back together. But Ferla took on the job, cleaning the mess, repairing the damage and rebuilding the dinner hall. This time, the hall was constructed directly across from where it had stood before, farther away from the water and made of steel and cement to withstand heavy winds. At a cost of over a quarter of a million dollars, the new structure was over three hundred feet long and one hundred feet wide and able to seat almost four thousand guests. Situated on a solid ledge foundation, its floor was raised twenty feet higher than that of the previous hall, to protect it from potential tidal waves. It was alleged that the new building could safely withstand winds up to two hundred miles per hour.

Efforts to return the park to its former status were in full force. Engagements were sought, exhibitions planned and events staged with gusto. In the summer of 1955, a call went out for all Rhode Island female co-eds between the ages of seventeen and twenty-four to enter the state's annual College Queen Beauty Contest. Information was available at Rocky Point's administration building, and the pageant would be held there at the park on August 25. The winner would go on to the national competition to be held at Ashbury Park, New Jersey, on September 9 and take a chance at winning $5,000 in prizes and scholarships, including an all-expenses-paid tour of Europe.

Time went on with the future unknown. In June 1959, the park's fortuneteller, Madam Tina, discovered that some thieving patron had stolen her crystal ball. The newspapers of the time joked that she probably didn't foresee the event.

The Shore Dinner Hall opened for business at noon, serving its famous chowder, clam cakes, watermelon and more until eight o'clock at night. The hall was carefully overseen by a host of waiters. In 1961, the all-you-can-eat chowder and clam cakes cost $1.10 for adults and $0.55 cents for children under the age of twelve.

Advertisements announcing "one hundred acres of fun" reached their intended audience. Rocky Point devotees returned to their beloved park, bringing new generations of thrill-seekers with them. The dimming light occasionally hinted at a new spark.

There were, however, bumps in the road. The park found its bingo license revoked in June 1961, when the Rhode Island Board of Public Safety decided to crack down on those who refused to follow the laws concerning a $700 limit on prizes. Rocky Point had been featuring games sponsored by a variety of different organizations, and it was discovered the park had given out twice the prize limit allowed. Park authorities argued that there was no way the games would maintain their popularity on a prize limit of $700. The Palladium, which could hold five thousand patrons, maintained its own license for holding bingo. Because the rules were followed within that building, their games, which were held three times a week, were allowed to go on.

Many organizations continued to use the park as the site for reunions, celebrations and recreation. One day that September, the grounds were reserved exclusively for the Palestine Temple Shriners, an ancient Arabic order.

With the addition of the Windjammer in 1966, famous bands and vocalists came to put on performances that drew an even greater number of visitors to Rocky Point. Band leader and violinist Guy Lombardo, bestselling female artist of the decade Patti Page and Frankie Lane of "Mule Train" fame were just a few of the big stars who traveled to Rhode Island to appear on the Rocky Point stage.

Still, the unexpected continued to occur. The park's Labor Day tradition was ruined that year when, at the beginning of August, vandals came into the park and torched the pile of debris that had been saved up for a bonfire.

Moving further into the twentieth century, the seaside resort had succeeded in regaining its reputation as the most tantalizing and titillating recreation destination in New England. The dinner hall, now the largest in the world, began filling to its capacity once more as visitors enjoyed the traditional fare along with baked sausage, broiled lobster and Indian pudding. So popular were the clam cakes and chowder that visitors begged in earnest for the recipe, which was kept a strict secret. John Balbina was among the new cooks at the park who worked hard at serving up edible perfection.

However, not everyone to visit Rocky Point gained the experience of a perfect outing. The gigantic swimming pool, which had been a major attraction since its construction in the 1930s, glistened with clear, cool salt water that was filtered in from the sea, and it was regularly crowded with folks of all ages, dipping in to cool off or projecting themselves from the diving boards that stood high above the pool. A terrible accident occurred in July 1967 when twenty-four-year-old Dale Kitchings of New York City was drowned on a Sunday afternoon after diving from one of the boards. He had been a member of the Play and Save Social Club, which had traveled to the park aboard seven busses to enjoy the day.

History continued to be made when famed classical composer Ron Nelson vacationed at the park that summer. He had been commissioned by Frank Bencriscutto to write a musical piece for an upcoming tour of Russia. Inspired by his seaside surroundings, Nelson composed a piece that he titled "Rocky Point Holiday."

In March 1969, Ferla sold Rocky Point to Budco Associates of New York. Later that year, New York resident Alvin H. Cohen purchased the park for $1.2 million, a far cry from the $1,200 sea captain William Winslow had paid for the property back in the previous century when it was merely a picturesque plot of land.

Cohen ended an annual tradition in 1970 that brought sadness to some but respect and gratitude from the chief of the Division of Air Pollution. The chief had previously criticized the annual bonfire that took place on the grounds each Fourth of July. Cohen understood the concern and said he was more than willing to help contribute to cleaner air by ceasing the bonfires at Rocky Point. There would be just one more, he explained, as debris for the event had been stacked up for months, and there was nowhere to dispose of the fifteen-foot-tall pile that covered three-fourths of an acre of parkland.

The large number of rides and amusements that now filled the resort included the new forty-five-foot-high flume, which carried passengers over a half mile of track; the castle of terror; bumper cars; a mini golf course; kiddy land; and a petting zoo. Over one hundred attractions and rides were available for enjoyment, and $3.00 got one a ticket to ride all day from noon to closing. The saltwater pool opened daily at ten o'clock in the morning, and the all-you-can-eat shore dinners were available for just $1.50 for adults and $0.80 for children. Entrance to the park was $0.50 per person.

The number of deaths at Rocky Point, unfortunately, continued to rise. In September of that year, an accident occurred that killed a navy Seabee. Thirty-two-year-old Edwin Walker was with the Twenty-first Naval

Rocky Point Park was a playground for adults and children alike. *Vintage postcard, courtesy Jules Antiques & General Store.*

Construction Regiment and living in Davisville, Rhode Island. After serving two terms in Vietnam, he was working part time as a maintenance man at the park. While repairing a cable guard pulley on the Skyliner, he stood on the large wheel that pulled the cable. Somehow, the ride started up, and he was pulled between the wheel and the base of the ride.

The park's boathouses and bathhouses dotted the shore along with the Ladies' Reception Room, the public water fountain, the flying horses, the bowling alley and the icehouse big enough to hold one thousand tons of ice. The resort continued to grow and prosper. Its life had been threatened and nearly ended on numerous occasions. But it had always been saved, resuscitated and returned to the people, bigger and better than it had been before. Eventually, Rocky Point gained its place in history as the second-oldest American amusement park in existence. A new mascot, in the form of a pirate, began to appear on the grounds. "Captain Rocky" entertained children and invited them to join his fan club. This dramatically costumed role was played for many years by Francis Szklany of Westerly.

In May 1977, Ronald Reagan arrived at Rocky Point on a political mission, speaking to a crowd of over four hundred people at a $100-per-plate fundraiser, and in August, visitors to the park enjoyed a nail-biting performance by Rietta Wallenda, whose family of aerialists was well known as the Flying Wallendas. Balancing on a tightrope 50 feet in the air without a net, the sixteen-year-old girl performed with three other family members at the park. Her famous grandfather Karl had been killed during a circus performance just a few months earlier in San Juan, Puerto Rico, when a strong gust of wind interfered with his balance; he fell 120 feet to his death.

In 1963, two family members had been killed and three others seriously injured during a performance at a Detroit fair. While showing off their famous seven-member pyramid, the high wire snapped and the pyramid collapsed, sending them all falling to the ground. Karl's forty-three-year-old sister-in-law was one of the two who were killed, and Rietta's uncle Mario was permanently paralyzed from the waist down with no chance of ever walking again. Later that same year, Yetta Wallenda, who was in her forties, fell to her death while performing at a circus in Omaha, Nebraska. Another family member also fell from the high wire and was killed during a circus performance in Wheeling, West Virginia.

On Thanksgiving Day 1980, a fire destroyed a row of game and concession stands located in the midway. The following year, two park employees were arrested on federal charges and served indictments handed down by a grand jury that charged them with setting the fire and thereby

Rocky Point Park - 1980's

Warwick Neck, Rhode Island

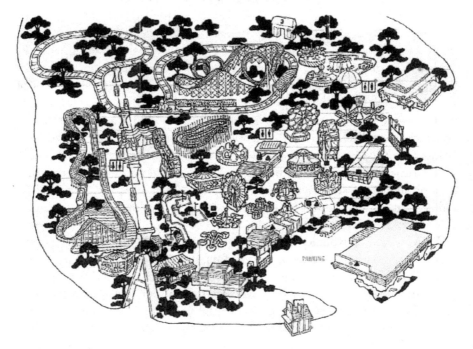

A 1980s map of Rocky Point Park, providing a guided tour of the grounds. *Author's collection.*

damaging property—which affected interstate commerce by the use of an explosive—as well as conspiracy. Police and fire investigators believed that the stands had been saturated with a flammable liquid before being set on fire. The two men pleaded innocent to the charges. Later, a trial resulted in one of the maintenance men being convicted of arson.

The year 1982 saw the construction of a new roller coaster, the Corkscrew, purchased for the park at a cost of $2 million. The ride was designed by Arrow Dynamics and provided a dramatic sixty-four-foot drop to those brave enough to climb aboard.

The arrival of the Cyclone, another new roller coaster designed by Arrow, came in 1983. The ride contained three vertical drops and two corkscrew loops, reaching speeds of over fifty miles per hour.

The Freefall, which was not for the faint of heart, was erected on the grounds in 1988, allowing riders the stomach-dropping sensation of quickly descending from a height of twelve and a half stories at fifty-five miles per hour. The ride had initially stood at another amusement park but lost its attraction when four teenagers were injured while riding it, even after new safety features were installed. This would be the last ride ever introduced at Rocky Point Park.

That same decade, it was decided that the Olympic-sized saltwater pool was simply too costly for the owners to keep in operation. The popular attraction that had been the scene of so much laughter and summertime fun was closed down and filled in.

By 1993, quite a bit had changed. The park was under new ownership and, like most things in life, didn't operate on pennies and dimes anymore. Admission to the grounds, no longer free of charge, required a payment of $2.95 per person. Admission with a ride-all-day ticket was priced at $13.95 for adults and children standing over four and a half feet tall. Those falling under that height paid just $8.95 cents.

The park opened at eleven o'clock in the morning, with the twenty-one rides and ten kiddy rides opening for business at noontime. Little did anyone know that the life support that had always managed to pull the park out of whatever dying state it fell into wouldn't be there to save it the next time disaster presented itself.

14

A FINAL END

In 2001, the U.S. Bankruptcy Court for the District of Rhode Island heard the case of Acropolis Enterprises Incorporated versus C.R. Amusements (also known as Rocky Point Amusement Park), James Callahan, Henry Vara, Rita Dimento and Francis Dimento. As the result of a dispute between shareholders, Acropolis had filed a complaint concerning determination of the extent, amount and priority of its lien against the debtor's assets, which secured a loan of $8,339,518.

During the 1980s, Rocky Point Park had been owned by Captain Rocky Incorporated, Rocky Point Amusements, Kiddy Park Incorporated and other entities. Their operations were financed by the Bank of New England. When the bank began to experience financial difficulties, it called in its note. Captain Rocky and its affiliates needed to quickly secure other financing and, in September 1991, began a lending relationship with Fairway Capital Corporation. Fairway loaned Captain Rocky $5,395,000 at 15.5 percent interest per year, to be made in payments over the course of twenty years but with a balloon payment due in five years. Under the agreement, Captain Rocky was required to pay interest of approximately $900,000 per year. To be able to do that, the park would have to escrow $50,000 per week during its open season. This obligation was personally guaranteed by Callahan, Vara and the Dimentos.

In 1994, the defendants defaulted on the loan, and Moneta Capital Corporation was placed into receivership. The loan was assigned to Participation Services Corporation, created by Arnold Kilberg to service the loan. Threatened with foreclosure, Captain Rocky and its associates filed for bankruptcy. Callahan, Vara and the Dimentos owned 100 percent of the shares of Captain Rocky. Captain Rocky also owned 100 percent of the shares of the affiliated companies. Callahan reported that the goal was to emerge free of personal guarantees on the Fairway loan, retain some equity interest in the park and eliminate personal liability on unpaid sales and payroll tax obligations.

The following year, attempts to secure food and game concessionaries for the park were unsuccessful. At that time, an agreement was made between Captain Rocky, Moneta Capital and Kilberg, who was the investment advisor for both Moneta and Fairway. Under the agreement, a reorganization plan was put into place that declared that Moneta would acquire the Fairway loan and that all unpaid interest, legal fees and late charges due under the original loan would be capitalized and added to the Moneta loan. In addition, the Moneta loan would be fully due in five years, and a new limited liability company would be created in which to transfer all Rocky Point assets—free of all liens except the Moneta mortgage—prior liens of record and the property tax lien. It was also agreed that Moneta would own 51 percent of the common membership interest of the new company, with Callahan, Vara and the Dimentos owning 49 percent.

Moneta was to receive a $1.5 million nonvoting-preferred-membership interest in the new company, and while Callahan, Vara and the Dimentos' personal guarantees would be released, they would remain jointly and severally liable to the new company for any payroll and sales tax liabilities paid by the new company on behalf of the former company.

In October of that year, the reorganization plan was accepted by the bankruptcy court in Worcester, and all the assets of Rocky Point were transferred to C.R. Amusements, which was to begin locating food, game and ride concessionaries who were willing to pay at least 20 percent of their gross revenues to C.R. Amusements.

Callahan, who had failed in this effort before, led the search. He, Vara and the Dimetos would later claim that Kilberg and Moneta made the task difficult by refusing to cooperate and by refusing to give them consent for certain concessionaires to be contracted. They stated that they believed Moneta never really intended to see the park in operation but secretly planned to eventually develop a large residential waterfront community on the property. Moneta's scheme, they charged, was to financially cripple C.R. Amusements so that it would be forced to default on its loan, allowing Moneta to acquire the property at foreclosure. It would then be able to develop the property and retain all financial gains for itself. Moneta's actions, as a 51 percent shareholder of C.R. Amusements, they claimed, was a breach of fiduciary duty.

When Callahan's efforts to secure concessionaries failed, C.R. Amusements was left with very little money from operations. In the winter of 1996, it was decided to sell the park's rides and equipment the following spring. Callahan, Vara and the Dimentos alleged that they had no involvement in the decision to sell the rides and that the sale was a unilateral, preplanned move by Moneta to dispose of the rides rather than operate the park so that it could develop the land instead. They further charged that Moneta insisted that, from the proceeds of the sale, $1.5 million would be paid to redeem its nonvoting preferred membership interest, five years earlier than agreed on.

The operating agreement, however, stated that Moneta had the authority to sell the rides with or without the consent of the other shareholders. It also stated that the business affairs of the company would be managed exclusively by Moneta's board of managers and that it would direct and control company business to the best of its ability. In addition, the agreement stated that Moneta had complete and full authority, power and discretion to make any and all decisions and to do any and all things that the board of managers deemed necessary to accomplish the business objectives.

A letter of agreement, dated January 2, 1996, was produced in which both parties had agreed to a liquidation of C.R. Amusement's assets and a payment of $1.5 million to Moneta from the proceeds of the sale. On January 30, 1996, C.R. Amusements contracted with Norton Auctioneers to schedule an auction at the park. All rides and equipment were to be sold on April 16 and 17 of that year.

Auction day was a day of despair not only for the park owners but also for all Rhode Islanders. For ten dollars, a color brochure of everything on the auction block could be had. Every ride, amusement, table and chair was sold before the deserted park's gates were locked. With the wind slicing the air and cold rain spitting down from the clouds, it was with great sadness that the crowd watched decades' worth of memories be cleared away. The Freefall, which had provided thousands with the scare of a lifetime, fetched $500,000 and found a new home in Ohio. The log flume was actually resold later in the day to the second-highest bidder and shipped to the Philippines. The Cyclone went to Canada. The famous Corkscrew found itself a new owner in Seattle, Washington, for the hefty price of $805,000. Immovable structures such as game stands and ride shelters were later razed or left to simply collapse.

Just prior to the start of the auction, several pieces of restaurant equipment, valued at about $300,000, were removed from the sale. Callahan, Vara and the Dimentos alleged that the equipment was removed by Kilberg without their input or approval. This action, they claimed, caused them to lose out on proceeds that they would have obtained from the sale of the equipment and cost them an auctioneer's commission of 8 percent and a buyer's premium of 5 percent, totaling $39,000, for equipment that was never sold. They also claimed that $693,650 worth of assets were purchased by C.R. Amusements from itself, as a man named Timothy DelGiudice, purportedly on behalf of C.R. Amusements, successfully bid on numerous items, including the flume ride, which went for $450,000.

Callahan, Vara and the Dimentos alleged that DelGiudice worked for Moneta and was being directed by Kilberg to bid on certain items. This, they stated, was flagrant misconduct by Moneta, which cost them a loss of over $307,000.

Moneta's people argued that they had no knowledge of DelGiudice bidding on items for the benefit of C.R. Amusements and that it had been a shock to later learn that C.R. Amusements had acquired the flume for $450,000. They claimed that DelGiudice actually worked for Vara and was bidding under his direction, as Vara wanted to keep the park open. Vara had been operating the Rocky Point Family Fun Fair on the grounds.

Proceeds from the auction totaled $3,049,050. The City of Warwick was paid $600,000 for delinquent real estate taxes. Moneta received $1.5 million pursuant to the January 2, 1996 agreement letter. The alternate plan, which was that of developing Rocky Point Park into real estate, was then begun.

On May 21, 1997, after C.R. Amusements had defaulted in mortgage payments, Moneta sent the company a notice of foreclosure. The property was to be put up for sale on July 3, 1997. Callahan, Vara and the Dimentos sought a temporary restraining order from the Providence County Superior Court, which was denied. Callahan then filed an involuntary bankruptcy petition against C.R. Amusements, averting the foreclosure sale.

On August 5, 1999, Callahan, Vara and the Dimentos had filed a motion to intervene as defendants. Once the majority shareholders entered the case, they filed a counterclaim against Acropolis, asking that the claim of Acropolis be equitably subordinated to the claims of the State of Rhode Island and the Internal Revenue Service for the payroll and tax liabilities assumed by the debtor as part of a prior bankruptcy case; the claim of Callahan for his professional fees and expenses generated as a result of the debtor's failure to pay payroll and sales tax liabilities; and the claim of Callahan, Vara and the

Dimentos for up to $1.5 million representing a return on their equity equal to the amount previously paid to Moneta Capital.

It was expected that the property would be sold that year for $10 million. However, it would be awhile before it found a new owner. On December 10, Moneta transferred and assigned its loan and security documents back to Participation Services. In February of the following year, that company assigned the loan and documents to Acropolis.

Acropolis sent a new notice of foreclosure to C.R. Amusements on March 18, 2000. Callahan, Vara and the Dimentos reacted by placing C.R. Amusements into state court receivership, and a Kent County judge enjoined Acropolis from proceeding with the foreclosure. Kilberg, as manager of Moneta, filed an instant voluntary bankruptcy petition.

The court addressed the issues of Callahan, Vara and Dimento regarding Moneta's alleged interference with their ability to obtain park concessions, Moneta's alleged improprieties during the auction and its acceleration of the redemption of the nonvoting preferred membership interest. The court did not feel that there was evidence to support any breach of fiduciary duty and decided that the minority shareholders had not sustained their burden of proof on other charges. Their counterclaim against Acropolis was denied and dismissed. The land and chaotic mass of fallen structures on the property were sold in 2003 for $8.5 million, with the winning bid coming from the United States Small Business Administration.

In the autumn of 2004, members of the Seaconke Wampanoag Indian tribe filed a lawsuit in which it claimed that several parcels of land in Rhode Island, by rights, belonged to it. Among those parcels was thirty-four acres of land within Rocky Point Park. The tribe's archivist, Peter Bauer, claimed that he had done a great deal of research at the Warwick Public Library and had discovered a 1661 deed, in the Nathanael Greene collection, that showed the Rocky Point land had been given to the tribe by the king of England.

The court ruled that such a claim could not be filed due to the Land Settlement Act of 1978, whereby 1,800 acres of land were conveyed to the Narragansett Indian tribe under the stipulations that no other Indian land claims could be made against the state or federal government for damages of lost use of aboriginal land unless such claims were brought forth within 180 days of the bill's being passed. The court reminded the tribe that the deadline was long since over. Bauer argued that the title on the land was not aboriginal; it was a recognized transfer by the king. In addition, he stated, it was unconstitutional for the Wampanoags to suffer such a loss based on a deal made with the Narragansett Indians, who were part of an entirely different tribe.

The two main tribes in possession of the shore lands situated along Narragansett Bay in 1636, when Roger Williams settled in Rhode Island, were the Wampanoags and the Narragansetts. The earliest written account of their presence there was by Giovanni da Verranzano in 1524. Among the first English settlements on the bay was the area now known as Warwick, and the colonists and thousands of Indians shared use of the land. It was the Indians, in fact, who showed the English how to dig for clams at low tide and how to prepare a clambake by producing steam from hot rocks and layers of seaweed.

Neither the Wampanoags, nor any other Indian tribe, would be allotted any part of the former park property.

The silenced land of the former resort, standing there like an enchanted ghost town, was a magnet for vandals as well as a fire hazard. On October 16, 2006, a blaze destroyed the Cliff House. The two-story wood-frame executive building, standing high atop a hill, was where the park's seasonal staff had once been housed. A boater had discovered the fire when he looked toward the park at approximately half past six o'clock in the evening and saw flames rising high into the sky.

The Rocky Point sign at the park's entrance, taken shortly before its demolition. *Photograph by Kelly Sullivan Pezza.*

The demolition of the midway took place in May 2007. On June 4, during the rainy early morning hours, the main entrance gate, emblazoned with the large "Rocky Point" sign, was demolished. On September 7, documentary film producer David Bettencourt introduced the world premiere of *You Must Be This Tall: The Story of Rocky Point Park* at the filled-to-capacity Stadium Theater in Woonsocket.

It was also that year that developer Nicholas Cambio backed out of a deal to construct a residential community on the property when he and the United States Small Business Administration could not agree on a payment schedule for the $19 million land. Vanderbilt Capital also backed out of a deal when its plans to build 396 condominiums, town houses and duplexes were not met favorably by the City of Warwick. The company, which was composed of a partnership between Toll Brothers builders and developer Arnold Goodstein, had the winning bid on the property at $25 million, more than double the amount that some other developers offered. But when the city expressed its concern over the proposed sewerage plans for a project of such a great size, the deal began to fall apart at the seams. Later, when the Small Business Administration determined that the buildings left on the property were a safety hazard and needed to be razed, it felt the cost of demolition should be carried by Vanderbilt. The friction landed both parties in court with an eventual agreement that Vanderbilt would pull out of the deal and allow the Small Business Administration to retain the company's initial $500,000 payment to finance the razing.

Later that year, the City of Warwick secured a federal grant of over $2 million, through the efforts of Senator Jack Reed, to purchase half the property. Another $2 million plus was funded by the state. The tract included wetlands and a one-mile stretch of land along the shore. The following October, nearly 2,500 people arrived one Sunday after an invitation went out for locals to come get a peek at what was soon to become a new state park.

In 2013, the remaining acreage was conveyed to the State of Rhode Island, with the Department of Environmental Management overseeing maintenance and development. The DEM went on to budget $2.5 million for a thorough cleanup of the property.

Veri/Waterman Associates was awarded the contract to develop a schematic master plan for a waterfront state park along forty-one acres of shoreline. Newport Collaborative Architects would serve as architectural consultants, and the plan was to preserve as many of the remaining park artifacts as possible with a focus on ecological, environmental and economic sustainability.

The Rocky Point Foundation, an organization of people dedicated to saving and preserving all they could of Rocky Point's history, had lobbied for state ownership of the property in 2010 and continued its efforts by fighting to save what remained of the park's observation tower and the aged skeletons of older rides that still stood on the land. Founded by Warwick Beacon publisher John Howell, the foundation showed great determination toward preserving the property for public use, as opposed to razing the land and constructing condominiums.

By the beginning of 2014, a major cleanup of the park was yet to be done. The bones of the shore dinners hall still stood, along with the rusted remnants of rides and the deteriorating Palladium. Graffiti and vandalism now mar the once beautiful resort, which is overgrown with weeds and bushes and strangled by vines.

People from around the country, especially those in New England, would long remember the carefree summer days they had spent at Rocky Point. Aside from the famous chowder and clam cakes, the bakes along the shore and the most thrilling rides to be found on the East Coast, the park had been the site of so many historic events and unforgettable moments.

The who's who of park patrons had grown steadily over the years, from famous sports figures to presidents and chart-topping vocalists to military heroes. John Jacob Astor had come to show crowds that even millionaires liked to have fun; John L. Sullivan wowed the masses with his brawn; and Janis Joplin, REO Speedwagon and the Red Hot Chili Peppers got patrons rocking. Year after year, decade after decade, century after century, it was proven that Rocky Point was a magnet for all that was important or entertaining.

Rhode Islanders still ache for pieces of the past. Online auctions rack up the bids for old Rocky Point bumper stickers, napkins, cups, ride tickets and T-shirts. Some even resort to stealing as a means of getting their hands on souvenirs. In 2013, the five-foot-tall fiberglass lobster standing outside the Green Pond Fish Market in Falmouth, Massachusetts, went missing. The lobster was one of many that had once been positioned around the grounds of Rocky Point as its logo. Standing erect on its tail, holding a cane in one hand and tipping its straw hat with the other, the lobster was synonymous with summer fun.

In addition to aged souvenirs, memories and photographs are what now remain; stories recalled and written down and visual images captured on paper and film are immortal pieces of Rhode Island history. They will never let the famous park's tale be forgotten, from its small beginnings, through its long life, to the slow, resistant move toward a final end.

At the present time, Rocky Point stands like a forgotten dream behind the wall of jagged rocks. Its gaiety and music have faded into the past. Its wharf slowly falls into the sea.

The property is simply a remnant of another time, when it was the place for thousands upon thousands of people to come and spend carefree summer days. And though it was rarely talked about, it was the place where one little girl spent her last frightening moments on this earth, surrounded by laughter and barrel organ melodies.

BIBLIOGRAPHY

Afro-American archives, Maryland, August 23, 1930.

Ancestry.com.

Assorted Rhode Island City directories.

Beaver County Times archives, Pennsylvania, August 30, 1978.

Belcher, Horace G. "Old Rocky Point." *Rhode Island History* (April 1948). Rhode Island Historical Society, Providence, Rhode Island.

Berkshire Eagle archives, Massachusetts, June 6, 1959.

Bettencourt, David, and Stephanie Chauvin. *Rocky Point Park*. Charleston, SC: Arcadia Publishing, 2009.

Bicknell, Thomas W. *The History of the State of Rhode Island and Providence Plantations*. New York: American Historical Society, 1920.

Cranston Town Hall death records.

Denison, Frederic. *The Past & Present: Narragansett Sea & Shore; An Illustrated Guide to Providence, Newport and Narragansett Pier*. Providence, RI: J.A. & R.A. Reid Publishers, 1880.

East Greenwich Pendulum archives, Rhode Island.

East Greenwich Preservation Society.

Evening Bulletin archives, Rhode Island, September 23, 2938.

Evening News archives, Rhode Island, 1862; July 23, 1891; 1893; July 17, 1909; August 7, 1909; August 14, 1909; August 21, 1909; September 4, 1909; September 13, 1909; April 7, 1910; June 25, 1910; July 17, 1909; July 19, 1909; December 23, 1910; May 27, 1911; June 10, 1911; June 17, 1911; June 24, 1911; July 1, 1911; July 5, 1911; May 18, 1912; June 22,

1912; June 29, 1912; July 15, 1912; August 10, 1912; August 17, 1912; May 29, 2913; June 18, 1913; June 28, 1913; July 3, 1913; July 12, 1913; July 25, 1913; July 26, 1913; August 1, 1913; August 2, 1913; August 4, 1913; August 16, 1913; August 18, 1913; August 24, 1913; August 30, 1913; October 22, 1913; May 4, 1914; May 27, 1914; June 20, 1914; July 3, 1914; July 4, 1914; July 18, 1914; July 24, 1914; August 1, 1914; June 30, 1917.

Familysearch.org.

Hale, Stuart O. *Narragansett Bay: A Friend's Perspective.* N.p.: for the University of Rhode Island Marine Advisory Service, 1980.

Hour archives, Connecticut, 1989.

Hurd, Henry Mill. *The Institutional Care of the Insane in the United States and Canada.* Baltimore, MD: John Hopkins Press, 1916.

Independent archives, Florida, June 14, 1918.

Langworthy Public Library.

Ledger archives, Florida, 1987.

Lewiston Journal archives, Maine, March 16, 1987.

Library of Congress.

Milwaukee Journal archives, Wisconsin, September 9, 1978.

Nashua Telegraph archives, New Hampshire, 1981.

New London Day archives, Connecticut, 1886; 1893; July 25, 1904; 1913; 1917; April 26, 1991; January 14, 1996; January 17, 1996; May 4, 1999; 2003; September 11, 2007; October 27, 2008.

Newport Daily News archives, Rhode Island, October 11, 1951; April 6, 1953; August 22, 1953; July 8, 1955; June 29, 1961; July 19, 1961; September 8, 1961; September 9, 1961; August 4, 1966; July 24, 2967; March 3, 1969; July 18, 1969.

Newport Mercury archives, Rhode Island, May 7, 1904; August 12, 1905; July 8, 1922.

News & Courier archives, South Carolina, 1914; January 31, 1957.

New York Times archives, New York, July 8, 1869; August 25, 1872; May 29, 1880.

Pawtuxet Valley Gleaner archives, Rhode Island.

Portsmouth Herald archives, New Hampshire, July 1, 1970; September 4, 1970.

Providence Journal archives, Rhode Island, May 30, 1948; January 30, 1949; March 27, 1955; November 7, 2003; September 3, 2004; December 30, 2006; January 31, 2007; May 28, 2013.

Providence Public Library.

Providence Superior Court Records Department.

Records of the United States Bankruptcy Court for the State of Rhode Island.
Rhode Island Heritage Hall of Fame archives.
Rhode Island Historical Cemeteries Transcription Project.
Rhode Island Historical Society.
Rhode Island Historic Preservation Commission reports.
Rhode Island State Archives.
Rhode Island Supreme Court Records Department.
Rootsweb.com.
Sarasota Herald Tribune archives, Florida, August 12, 1977.
Soares, Joseph P. *Westerly Postcard History*. Charleston, SC: Arcadia Publishing, 2006.
Society for American Baseball Research. Baseball Biography Project.
Stonington Town Hall birth, death and marriage records.
Telegraph archives, New Hampshire, May 20, 1977.
University of Rhode Island Library newspaper archives.
Utter, Herbert. *Old Pictures of Westerly, Rhode Island*. Westerly, RI: Utter Publishing Company, 1991.
Warwick Beacon archives, Rhode Island, 1893; September 7, 2004; September 14, 2004.
Warwick City Hall death records.
Warwick Historical Society.
Warwick Public Library.
Westerly Sun archives, Rhode Island, 1893.
Wikipedia.org.
www.earlyaviators.com.
www.findagrave.com.
www.wilmerhale.com.
www.windrep.org.

ABOUT THE AUTHOR

Kelly Sullivan Pezza is a native of Hope Valley, Rhode Island, and has worked as a journalist for Southern Rhode Island Newspapers for seventeen years. With an education in law enforcement and many years of experience as a Rhode Island historian and genealogist, she has written hundreds of articles and several books concerning historic true crime and unsolved mysteries in Rhode Island.

In addition to her works of nonfiction such as *History, Mystery & Lore of Rhode Island*, the author has also published two fictional dramatic novels: *Snowglobe* and *The Rarest Beautiful*.

The winner of the Kraft National Writing Award and the New England Press Award, she provided a portion of the historical narration for the acclaimed documentary *You Must Be This Tall: The Story of Rocky Point*, produced by documentary filmmaker David Bettencourt in 2007.

Currently, she is at work on her third fictional novel and continues to seek out stories of the unnerving, the unexpected and the unfathomable.

CPSIA information can be obtained
at www.ICGtesting.com
Printed in the USA
LVHW050900190723
752643LV00051B/11